EDUCATION FOR
CRIME PREVENTION
AND CONTROL

CRIMINAL LAW EDUCATION
AND
RESEARCH CENTER

Publications of the Criminal Law
Education and Research Center

Volume 10

New York University
School of Law

EDUCATION FOR CRIME PREVENTION AND CONTROL

Edited by

ROBERT JOE McLEAN, ESQ.

Criminal Law Education and Research Center Fellow
New York University School of Law

With an Introduction by

Gerhard O. W. Mueller

Professor of Law
Director, Criminal Law Education and Research Center
New York University

166164

HV
6024
.E 37

CHARLES C THOMAS · PUBLISHER
Springfield · Illinois · USA

ST. JOSEPH'S UNIVERSITY   STX

HV6024.E37
Education for crime prevention and contr

3 9353 00000 3762

Published and Distributed Throughout the World by

CHARLES C THOMAS • PUBLISHER

Bannerstone House

301-327 East Lawrence Avenue, Springfield, Illinois, U.S.A.

This book is protected by copyright. No part of it
may be reproduced in any manner without written
permission from the publisher

© 1975, by CHARLES C THOMAS • PUBLISHER

ISBN 0-398-03226-2

Library of Congress Catalog Card Number: 74-8182

*With THOMAS BOOKS careful attention is given to all details of
manufacturing and design. It is the Publisher's desire to present books that
are satisfactory as to their physical qualities and artistic possibilities and
appropriate for their particular use. THOMAS BOOKS will be true to those
laws of quality that assure a good name and good will.*

Printed in the United States of America
C-1

Library of Congress Cataloging in Publication Data
Main entry under title:

Education for crime prevention and control.

(Publications of the Criminal Law Education and
Research Center, v. 10)
"[Papers presented] on the occasion of the annual
congress of the American Society of Criminology, in
1972."
    1. Crime and criminals—Study and teaching—United
States—Congresses. 2. Criminal justice, Administra-
tion of—Study and teaching—United States—Congresses.
I. McLean, Robert Joe, ed. II. American Society of
Criminology. III. Series: New York University.
Criminal Law Education and Research Center. Publica-
tions, v. 10.
HV6024.E37   364'.07   74-8182
ISBN 0-398-03226-2

INTRODUCTION

O N THE OCCASION of the Annual Congress of the American Society of Criminology, in 1972, 15 of America's leading educators in the field of criminology and criminal justice offered their views and exchanged their experiences on how to solve the nation's crime and criminal justice problems by educating the appropriate number of specialists in the most appropriate manner and by then placing them in the field. What the 15 educators envisaged is an educational alternative to the efforts of the past which all too often aimed at a solution of the crime problem by sheer increase in the number of crime fighters or by a mere increase of technological capacity.

The papers in this volume, thus, represent the most advanced, current thinking in the field of education for crime prevention and control. In its three parts, the volume endeavors to offer an overview over the objectives of criminological education, an insight into the range of educational efforts within the criminal justice system, and, lastly, a projection of criminology into the total structure of higher and advanced education.

The search for solutions to America's crime problems is on. The emphasis is clearly on education. There will be many future research projects and action programs in the field of criminological education. May this volume open the door to a bright future.

G.O.W.M.

CONTENTS

vii

PART THREE—THE EXPANDING ROLE OF CRIMINOLOGICAL EDUCATION

EDUCATION FOR
CRIME PREVENTION
AND CONTROL

PART ONE

OBJECTIVES OF A CRIMINOLOGICAL EDUCATION

THE UNIVERSITY AND THE CRIMINAL JUSTICE SYSTEM: PARTNERS FOR A SCIENCE OF CRIMINOLOGY

——————— CHARLES L. NEWMAN, D.P.A. ———————

Professor Newman is Coordinator, Law Enforcement and Corrections Services and Professor of Law Enforcement and Corrections College of Human Development, The Pennsylvania State University, University Park, Pennsylvania. Professor Newman is also a past President of the American Society of Criminology.

INTRODUCTION

IT HAS BEEN A TRADITION of the American Society of Criminology for the President, as he leaves office, to offer some thoughts regarding the status of criminology, its past, present, or future.

I have been an active member of this society for two decades and have lived through its growing pains and emergence as a leading professional organization. It is with considerable pride that I look at our journal, editorially born in the basement of my home as "Criminologica," brought through "adolescence" by our past president, Professor Simon Dinitz, and now under the capable direction of Professor C. Ray Jeffery. I can well recall the continuing problem of maintaining financial solvency and the efforts of past president Conal MacNamara to sustain the organization. During the 1950's and 60's, such outstanding scholars and past presidents of the American Society of Criminology as Walter Reckless, Marvin Wolfgang, Bruno Cormier, Albert Morris, and Gerhard Mueller added to the growth and made their imprint on the organization.

Twice during the 1960's, our organization met in Canada. The decade of the 70's will be marked by our emerging partnership with professional colleagues throughout the Western Hemisphere and ultimately the world community. Directly and indirectly many scholars and universities have contributed time and effort to the growth of our organization, and with their continued help, we shall grow and make contributions to a science of criminology.

We have learned that scholarship, like justice and human dignity, cannot be bound by the constraints of national boundaries. Our search for truth and knowledge shares a tradition of centuries. Although the pursuit of knowledge and implementation may differ in form, the goals of understanding and justice are common to all of us.

It is, therefore, quite appropriate that this world assemblage of scholars and professionals from the various disciplines representative of the administration of justice should be meeting here in Venezuela. Our objectives are of the highest order: the exchange of ideas, the debate of philosophies, the consideration of techniques for the provision of criminal justice services. This convocation has provided the opportunity for teachers, researchers, administrators, and practitioners to expand the horizons of knowledge.

LACK OF INTERDISCIPLINARY CRIMINOLOGY

There is nothing particularly unique in a congress which brings together persons from any single discipline—criminology, sociology, psychology, law, or medicine—to discuss problems using the frame of reference of that discipline. What is unique is that representatives of all these disciplines are meeting together at this congress to consider the problems of law, society, and the offender from multidisciplinary and interdisciplinary perspectives. This approach represents a major departure from the usual conference format. This approach can begin to point the way for changes in our educational methodologies which traditionally have been compartmentalized within the confines of established disciplines.

The time-established boundaries that have prevailed between legal, medical, social science, and behavioral science education have neither enhanced the levels of scholarship nor motivated students to explore beyond those boundaries. When interdisciplinary efforts were established in the past, it was only by the activities of unusual individuals who were willing to risk the loss of disciplinary identity or who were willing to risk the stigma of not being a *real* member of a parent discipline.

The reluctance of scholars to take on interdisciplinary roles (except for short periods of expediency when research funding dictates working with other disciplines) is manifested in the criminological field by the lack of theory which is integrative rather than particular. The law violator is at once a biosocial individual living in a society of laws, values, and responsibilities. Yet, our theories do not portray the offender as a total person, but rather from the perspective of genetic misconstruction, superego malformation, opportunity blockage, peer malinfluence, economic deprivation, or discrimination.

As a criminologist whose experience has bridged both work in the field and the academic community, I am deeply concerned about the analysis of mechanisms which prepare personnel to operate criminal justice systems effectively. In recent years I have noted that my concerns are shared by many who have come to recognize the critical need for professionally qualified persons to manage the machinery of criminal justice—police, court services, corrections. Regrettably few universities have sponsored the necessary criminal justice education programs.

The issue is not as simplistic as the reluctance of universities to "train" technicians for government coupled with a commitment to educate scholars. The unwillingness of universities to accept a training responsibility is deep-rooted and springs from historical conceptions of the role of the university which, in effect, stated that "to be scholarly, one must reject any on-going relationship with the systems of government, its personnel, or its problems." Where liaisons have been established between university and agency for such specific purposes as student research, the relationships have been less than satisfactory to both groups.

ESTABLISHING PARTNERSHIPS

There are certainly many reasons why criminological partnerships have not been effectively established between academic and criminal justice field-based personnel. The critical element is that such partnerships *must* be developed. In a variety of areas, universities have been the focal point for the accumulation of specific knowledge and skills developed to apply rational approaches to major sets of problems. In this sense, the tenacity of crime and delinquency represents a legitimate arena for scholarly study as well as for the rational development of action programs to provide solutions.

Knowledge for What?

The description of the problem may well be the most simple portion of the overall task. This may explain the plethora of scholarly works which decry the state of the social environment or describe, in global or minute terms, the historical, genetic, biosocial, or environmental condition of the offender. In some instances these descriptions with refined statistical manipulation do indeed provide an accurate picture of the person or events under consideration. But this specialized knowledge does not carry with it any action dimension or any prescription for behavior modification. It is in this latter area that we as scholars have failed, and it in part accounts for the fact that criminology has been viewed with scorn by those on the action level. I am not in anyway suggesting that there is only one action possibility for any given set of events. What I am saying is that, as criminologists, we have tended to ignore the potentials for action which stem from our inquiries. Nor have we suggested alternate conceptual models around which action programs can be developed. Research, we would all agree, is the mechanism by which knowledge is accumulated. The question I am raising here is "Knowledge for What?"

Some would be satisfied to respond that our accumulation of knowledge is a legitimate end in itself. In those decades when the university could isolate itself from the reality of the world's problems, the luxury of such monastic inquiry could be sustained. This kind of world no longer exists.

CRIMINOLOGY'S THREE-FOLD RESPONSIBILITY

It is my position that criminology, as a part of the larger society, has a three-fold responsibility. This responsibility can optimally be fulfilled in a joint effort between the educational institutions and the various sub-fields of practice. The three areas of criminological responsibility are research, education, and staff development. I have spoken of *research* as the mechanism for the analysis of systems and individual characteristics producing both crime and its control.

Education is the second area of attention. A problem so persistent and universal as crime depends upon personnel with unique configurations of specific knowledge and skills, *education*. I have suggested that the university has a major role in criminological education which only recently has begun to be fulfilled. More often than not, in the past this university participation has been limited to criminology as appendages to pre-existing academic departments. Criminologists are frequently viewed either with suspicion or are ignored by the established disciplines. Interdisciplinary activities rarely occur.

In my judgment, there is a critical need for the development of independent faculties of criminology with the autonomy to develop broad-based interdisciplinary activities in pursuit of new criminological knowledge. These faculties would also provide sound educational programs at the undergraduate as well as the graduate levels for students who ultimately can enter as creative and contributing participants in criminal justice systems. Time does not permit a detailed elaboration of the strategies which can be utilized in designing such an educational program (Newman, 1971). Suffice it to say, at this point a critical need exists in every country for personnel with specific knowledge and necessary action skills to make criminal justice systems work. It is reasonable to suggest that the failures in relation to crime control and behavior modification strategies lie in the criminal justice system as it relates to the larger society. Further, we have attempted a fragmented approach to the personnel situation by superimposing individuals with exposure to university dispensed information on a system which questions the reality and value of university-generated knowledge. Obviously, there is much room for the strengthening of ties between the academic community and the criminal justice segments of society.

The third concern of criminology which must be developed

involves a direct *staff development* relationship by universities to shape the talents and skills of those persons already employed in criminal justice occupations. An obvious benefit to the system is that the working personnel will have an opportunity to become more receptive to the products of university education. Moreover by direct participation in training efforts with agency personnel, the credibility of scholars can also be enhanced since they will be directly involved in the field upon which they seek to have a direct impact. With personnel in the field more sensitive to the university role in knowledge production, a greater receptivity to research procedures and processes should ultimately emerge. Critically, then, criminal justice agencies and their staffs will develop an appreciation, in some cases for the first time, of the need for the development of new hypotheses, new postulates, and ultimately new theory about the nature, control, and defense measures related to crime and delinquency.

Conclusion

We are long past the time when we can continue the isolation of the criminal justice field from the university. We must function together, and the mechanism which can forge such a partnership is a faculty of criminology which is broad-based in terms of function, interdisciplinary in terms of theoretic reference, and involved with the criminal justice system as researchers, teachers, planners, and consultants.

The direction I have proposed can bring us closer to a science of criminology, and I commend it to your consideration.

REFERENCE

Newman, C. L.: *Personnel Practices in Adult Parole Systems.* Springfield, Charles C Thomas, 1971.

CHAPTER 2

TOWARDS REFOCUSING CRIMINOLOGY

JAMES M. HENSLIN

Professor Henslin is a member of the Department of Sociology, Southern Illinois University, Edwardsville, Illinois.

THE FIELD OF CRIMINOLOGY is marked by disagreements. I am not simply referring to disagreements due to a lack of what we might call "master theory," or to differences in conceptualizing, nor to the lack of agreement regarding the etiology of crime, or even to varying contentions concerning the best method of preventing crime. Of such disagreements there appears to be no end. I am, rather, referring primarily to the lack of consensus regarding the proper subject matter of criminology (Wheeler, 1962; Quinney, 1970).

In addition to this disagreement over fundamentals, as well as the related differential defining of the field (e.g. Sutherland and Cressey, 1966; Wolfgang, 1963), criminologists have also been expressing a feeling that something is basically wrong with criminology as it is currently practiced. A major theme running through the writings of those who have expressed themselves on this matter is that criminologists have been overly preoccupied with offenders, to the neglect of more basic, and potentially more fruitful, concerns.

This more basic concern is the study of law itself, the analysis of how law comes into being, the process of which particular behaviors come to be labelled as criminal (Quinney, 1970; Sutherland and Cressey, 1966; Vold, 1958; Jeffery, 1959; Turk, 1964). I am not referring to the labelling of individuals, for a large and continuously growing body of literature surrounds this phenomenon (e.g. Becker, 1963; Lemert, 1951; Chiricos, Jackson and Waldo, 1972). Rather, I am referring to the lack of emphasis in criminology on the analysis of the conditions under which criminal law develops such that particular *behaviors* come to be pro-scribed by law. This situation is such a generalized tendency in criminology that even those who make such observations and lament the lack of emphasis on the conditions under which crim-inal law develops typically neglect it in their own works. Suther-land and Cressey (1966), for example, observe that seldom are the conditions under which criminal laws develop even included in general books on criminology. However, following this ob-servation, they only briefly mention the topic themselves, and that primarily in just the first few pages of their classic criminol-ogy text.

The "offender orientation" is such a part and parcel of crim-inology that in 1959 it was noted to characterize "every theory of criminal behavior which is discussed in the textbooks" (Jeffery, 1959). In 1970 Quinney observed that greater focus was being placed on "crime as a legal definition that is imposed upon hu-man activity by agents of the society charged with the formula-tion and administration of criminal law" (Quinney, 1970). This would tend to indicate that the emphasis is shifting, but on ex-amination it turns out that if there is such a shift it is almost imperceptible. Of the fifteen sources which Quinney cites to support his observation, approximately ten deal with the police or aspects of the enforcement of laws. The focus has perhaps increasingly turned towards the application of criminal law, dealing with such phenomena as differential enforcement, police discretion, and the like. But even in such studies *the existence of the law is typically taken as a central "given."* It is the rare study which takes the law itself as problematic. Three major excep-tions which deserve to be singled out are studies by Hall (1935, 1952), Radzinowicz (1948, 1957), and Turk (1964). Turk's study is especially deserving for its critical qualities.

This emphasis on the offender in criminology leads to the pursuance of many topical areas: crime rates, the ecology of crime, "criminal areas," criminal careers, labelling, norm deflec-tion, the criminal justice system, the administration of the law, differential enforcement patterns, courts, sentencing, penology, parole, probation, prevention, treatment, and the search for those casual, and fashionable, factors of criminal behavior, e.g. race, sex, "culture areas," poverty, the urban environment, broken homes, and the psychological and psychiatric variables. In all of this the law is accepted as a "given," with criminologists typically focusing on those who find themselves either on the administering or receiving end of the law.

Because of this emphasis in criminology as it is currently defined and practiced, criminology contains a built-in bias. This bias is extremely conservative in nature. Not making the law itself problematic results in criminologists adhering "to a status quo position, that is, accepting law and society as they exist" (Quinney, 1970). This conservative bias in criminology has rarely been more strongly phrased than in the following statement:

> The objective of criminology is the development of a body of general and verified principles and of other types of knowledge regarding this process of law, crime, and treatment or prevention. This knowledge will contribute to the development of other sciences and through these other social sciences it will *contribute to efficiency in general social control* (emphasis added) (Sutherland and Cressey, 1966).

This quotation is not meant by its authors as a criticism directed against criminology. They simply present it as a straightforward account of the objective of criminology, but to hold the development of principles of human behavior and knowledge as a means to "contribute to efficiency in general social control" as the objective of criminology is, at the very least, a highly conservative bias.

Central to conservatism, I believe, is the desire for people to follow normative structures, to obey the rules, and to bring pressures to bear on those who do not act in the expected manner. Conservatism tends to contain within it the desire to control others. Thus we note that at least half the contents of criminology texts deal with the prevention and control of crime (Quinney, 1970). We even find a book carrying the title *Controlling Delinquents* (Wheeler, 1968). Basic to this book is the idea that "there are systematic types of delinquents requiring different forms of treatment and control" (Wheeler, 1968). What is "required" is treatment (the assumption, I presume, is that something is "wrong" with these persons; they are felt to need treatment) and control (based, I presume, on the idea that such persons are either uncontrolled or improperly controlled). To take as one's goal the control of delinquents may very well require replacing their normative system, which may be law-breaking in type, with another normative system, one more accepting of legal codes (cf., Hindelang, 1970).

This conservative bias in criminology becomes apparent not only by examining the typical topics covered in introductory texts in criminology, by the subject matter of most graduate courses in criminology, or by the type of research in which most criminologists are engaged, but also by the "themes" of annual meetings of associations of criminologists. For example, this orientation is revealed most strongly in the first theme of our Interamerican Congress of Criminology: Criminological Perspectives in Social Defense. The subparts of this theme as given in the preliminary program read: (A) perspectives of prevention, (B) perspectives of crime control and deterrence, (C) perspectives of treatment, rehabilitation, and reintegration, and (D) perspectives of prediction methods. To prevent, control, deter, treat, rehabilitate, reintegrate, and predict appear to this analyst to be rather conservative in nature.

Underlying such orientations in criminology seems to be the idea that to prevent crime is to "strengthen" society. But to strengthen society without changing the existing social order, without overcoming present social inequalities, means to buttress the status quo by our activities, to reaffirm the power alignments as they now exist. To take one of the most obvious cases from these subparts of the theme, I assume that to "reintegrate" means to make the offender a part of the ongoing social system, to change him from an "antisocial" orientation. Again, to "reintegrate" an individual, in the absence of changing the inequalities of society, carries with it the idea of strengthening or solidifying the present social order.

By such an approach, criminologists run the risk of becoming not only identified with the oppressors, but becoming instruments of oppression themselves by siding with and becoming intertwined with the status quo. Support of the status quo, as I see it, means to maintain the gaps between the social classes. It is not surprising, then, that the "intellectual experts" of society have been called "the servants of those in power." They typically use their "assemblage of theory, concepts, skills and social legitimacy" to "define and manipulate meanings at the public's expense" (Manning, 1970).

Although there is really no end to the issues that are raised when one brings up a hypothetical situation, I think that it is enlightening for our own situation to raise the issue of what criminologists would be doing if they were performing their studies in Nazi Germany and were following what is now common practice in criminology. Granted that they were following what is now typical practice, what would they be researching? What would their approach imply for social control? Would they not still be studying those who violate the rules, since basic to their orientation would be taking "the law" for granted? More specifically, would they not be studying such persons as those who failed to report the whereabouts of Jews? Might not their studies, then, include learned theoretical treatises on how to make such persons conform, how to "reintegrate" them into society such that they conform to the laws and report "illegal persons"? Studies might also be done, of course, on the results of different sentencing procedures for such persons, and, of course, much speculation would follow regarding their recidivism rate.

Is this so farfetched as it sounds? I think not—granted the supposition that criminologists would be taking the law for granted, as is typically the case now. They would then be studying the results of law-breaking, rather than focusing on lawmaking and on the relationships between lawmaking and the different social groups within a society.

Placing the emphasis on the offender, with its concomitant conservativism, signifies, among other things, that the crimes of the privileged and powerful are not a focal concern in criminology. They are, in fact, noted not by their presence, but by their absence. When criminology is conceptualized as a discipline which deals with crime, and crime is narrowly circumscribed to mean acts of breaking the law, then the acts of those who are in a position to make and manipulate laws seldom come under study by the criminologist.

Something is drastically wrong with criminology, as it is currently conceived and practiced, when major criminal conspiracies involving the subversion of constitutional rights and the killing and maiming of literally hundreds of thousands of humans do not, by definition, come under the perusal of criminologists. McNamara, as secretary of defense, *planned* the bombing of peasants, the wholesale slaughter of civilians. Following his "work" he was promoted to the presidency of the International Bank for Reconstruction and Development, the prestigious and internationally influential World Bank. President Johnson, in following these plans of death, *gave orders* which resulted in hundreds of thousands of casualties. He later "retired" to part of his fifteen thousand acres in Texas. Although Johnson has passed from the public eye, his continuing power was again made visible before his death with the pilgrimage to Johnson by the aspirant to political power, George McGovern, during his 1972 presidential campaign. General Westmoreland *executed* Johnson's bombing orders, not just once but hundreds of times. For his efforts in this slaughter he was promoted to what is, in many ways, the single most powerful position in the United States outside of the Presidency, the Army Chief of Staff. Although President Nixon assured the American public during his 1968 campaign for the Presidency that he had a "secret plan" to end the war in Vietnam, following his ascendancy to power, he *continued* to give orders similar to Johnson, resulting in several hundred thousand more casualties. In spite of these acts, Nixon was allowed to again run for the Presidency (cf., Hughes, 1964).

Such events are not limited to the United States, although their magnitude for contemporary times may well be. I am focusing on them because I am more intimately familiar with events in the United States than elsewhere. Similar acts, however, are perpetrated by the elites of power and wealth in each of the countries which are variously represented by the participants in this Interamerican Congress of the American Society of Criminology and the Interamerican Association of Criminology.

In countries other than the United States such events usually occur on a much smaller scale (and with different specifics, of course), not because of differences in morality, but because of differences in power. One might cite any number of examples to support this position, but to simply choose one which has recently made the news, we can note the torture of political prisoners taking place at the direction of Mexico's power elite (Johnson, 1971). Regarding this latter situation, although it is now well publicized that political prisoners are being tortured in Mexico, these and similar acts probably will not be studied as criminal acts by Mexican criminologists, although delinquents among the poverty stricken class will probably continue to be so defined and so studied.

If such acts as I have outlined above are not crimes, then I propose that something is radically wrong with the definition of crime as it is currently employed by criminologists. I suggest that it is high time for us to forge a new definition of crime, one which is inclusive of such acts, as was done at the Nuremberg War Trials when it was found that the ordinary conceptions of criminal acts did not apply. The revelation of acts committed by men in power in Nazi Germany stirred the world. People could not understand how such highly "civilized" people could be guilty of such behavior. Today, however, citizens of the United States find that it is their own nation that is doing these same things. I would suggest that criminologists focus on acts as current, as large-scale, and as socially acceptable as those now being perpetrated by the power elite. The study of such acts should become a regular part of criminology, as much, certainly, as is the study of criminal acts by the lower classes. Such refocusing will allow us to examine the "institutionalization of crime" as it occurs, as it becomes part of the *Weltanschauung* of a people, as people's ideas are changed such that acts like these become part of the "normal" or "usual" way of thinking for a nation. We can also focus on the means by which dissenters are "exposed," prosecuted, persecuted, and in various ways discredited, as with Benjamin Spock, Angela Davis, the Berrigans, William Kunstler, and Daniel Ellsberg.

As we undergo a process of greater sensitization to the way

power is gained, administered, and maintained, and perhaps as we also undergo a process of disenchantment, of less belief in our governmental systems, we are better able to stand apart from our socio-politico-legal system, better able to examine them critically without merely taking their existence for granted. By making problematic much of that which we now take for granted, certain aspects of social life will become more visible to us, and, consequently, will be available for analysis (cf., Ichheiser 1970). We will be able to question the bases of power, as well as the uses to which power is put, and not simply continue to examine those who are on the receiving end of power—even though positions represented by that power are written into "law." Perhaps in such a way we can take steps towards what has been called the "new criminology" (Costner, 1971).

This brings us to the question of what the concerns would be in such a refocused criminology. In much of what I have just covered I have already indicated directions which a refocused criminology might take. More specifically, I see the following six focal concerns for the "new criminology."

1. The Social Origins of Laws

We need more historical studies in depth of the social origins of laws, such as those by Jeffery (1957), Hall (1935; 1952) and Radzinowicz (1948; 1957). For those of us who are from countries where our body of law was originally based on English law, the direction to take is obvious. Related questions involve legal transformation. How did we get from the laws we inherited to the body of law that we have today? What has been the relationship between conflict and consensus in the formulation of these laws? What social groups were most significant in formulating our laws? What was their relationship to other social groups at that time?

2. The Relationship of Law to the Maintenance of Power

Since power and authority is differentially distributed in society, basic questions should center on how law is used to maintain the positions of those who have power and authority. Ultimately, we should examine ways in which law-breaking is an attempt to redistribute power (cf., Schervish, 1971). What is the difference between "political" and "nonpolitical" crime? The slowness of the investigation by the United States Justice Department controlled by President Nixon following the bugging of the opposition party's headquarters by some of President Nixon's campaign workers is, I believe, such an example of the law being used to maintain power (cf., the editorial in the *Louisville Courier-Journal*, August 30, 1972).

3. The Relationship of Law and Power in the Maintenance of Meaning Systems

There are probably few of us who would disagree with the statement that "the political groups concerned with the creation and maintenance of power seek to construct political meanings which will constrain a populace to believe such meanings in fact represent a set of consistent political values" (Manning, 1970). In spite of the diverse meanings available in a pluralistic society with its various ethnic and minority worlds, its institutional and occupational worlds, how do some groups manage to gain the ascendency of their meaning system over others? What is the interconnection between law and the meaning system of those in power? Since groups, once having gained power, tend to utilize the law to their own advantage to consolidate their power, to maintain their position, and to stave off elements in society which threaten their position, what is the relationship between such goals and activities of those in power with the police, courts, and the lawmaking apparatus? How do those who are in power use the law and related symbolic manipulations to legitimate their ascent to power and to co-opt other segments of society? What is the relationship of such activities to stabilizations of the political order?

4. The Role of Violence in Establishing Laws

Perhaps a good start in this direction is the following statement: "Men seeking to seize, hold, or realign the levers of power have continually engaged in collective violence as part of their struggles. The oppressed have struck in the name of justice, the privileged in the name of order, those in between in the name of fear" (Tilly, 1969). What is the relationship between law and collective violence?

5. The Role of the Police in Repressing Those Who Wish to Alter the Social Order

This area is, of course, integrally related to the second, third, and fourth focal concerns mentioned above. Questions in this area would involve how the police are socialized into the values of those in power, as well as how they carry out these values. For example, since in the United States "whiteness" is a major value in social relationships, what is the relationship of racial prejudice to various aspects of law enforcement, such as the policeman's role? Is such prejudice purposely fostered among the police, whether overtly or covertly? Similar questions should be asked concerning other major values in a society (cf., Skolnick, 1970; Walker, 1968). For example, does subscribing to the values dominant in a society make the police a more willing instrument for repression?

6. The Administration of the Law

This area is, of course, directly related to the immediately preceding focal concern. How does the relationship between the legal superstructure and those in power affect the administration of law? What are "the rules for implementing the legal rules?" How do social control agencies function to pattern the risks for different groups in society? How do social control agencies relate to those who are least able to insulate themselves from their controlling activities?

Having suggested directions that the refocusing of criminology might take, I would like to seriously ask the question whether alternatives to our present emphasis are even possible. This involves two basic questions: (1) Is it not perhaps suicidal to change the emphasis and, (2) if it is not suicidal, do we really want such a change?

On the one hand, it may be suicidal to even attempt such a change. Such a refocus involves challenging the power structure. Challenging the power structure could very well mean bringing repression down on our own heads. Retaliation in modern political structures is ordinarily not as blatant as it once was. It is, however, still present, and it still comes in a direct physical sense: witness the plight of Kenneth Johnson, the political scientist from the United States who, because he wrote about electoral fraud in Mexico, the torture of political prisoners, and governmental control of the press by means of a monopoly on newsprint, was *detained* with his wife and child in jail for four days, threatened with physical harm, and expelled from Mexico (Johnson, 1971; *St. Louis Post-Dispatch*, August 24, 25, 28, 1972; and private communication with the author). In countries such as the United States, where totalitarianism is more masked, repression is also more masked, but it is nonetheless present. It seems that the greater the level of totalitarianism, the more direct the retaliation for criticizing the establishment.

If repression were not brought down on ourselves personally, and it certainly might be, then surely an "association of criminology," which had such an emphasis, would be viewed with hostility by the establishment. It would probably come into disrepute. At the minimum it would be viewed with suspicion. Funding, except for the areas those in power wanted investigated, would, I am sure, quickly dry up. Can criminology continue without such funding? Are alternative sources of funding available?

On the other hand, do we even want criminology to take a different direction? Criminologists who are in the university, for example, have a vested interest in maintaining pipelines to finances and other support in order to continue their research, to insure their publications, and thus to assure both their positions in the university and their professional prestige. This is indeed much to risk. But by asking if we desire such a change I am referring to something perhaps even more basic. In spite of the prevailing professional view that deviance (criminality) does not inhere in the act, that behaviors are not in and of themselves deviant (criminal), but are deviant (criminal) only as they are reacted to as such by others (Becker, 1963), I seriously wonder whether we really believe this (cf., Liazos, 1972). I wonder if we are not ourselves so strongly socialized into middle class values, values which perhaps ultimately uphold the political system, as well as protecting our own place within it, that we feel there is something inherently wrong with acts such as rape, murder, robbery, lying, cheating, and so on. And, accordingly, we study such offenders at least partially because their acts are offensive to us. It appears almost impossible for us to be other than ethnocentric, to not view our own behavioral characteristics or at least those subscribed to by our typical reference groups as *inherently* superior, which means in this case that we probably view not raping, not killing, not stealing, and so forth, as inherently superior traits. Such values are driven deeply into us at such an early age and are also so consistently reinforced over such a long period of our lives that I wonder if it is possible for us to ever think anything else. From associating with professionals, and from knowledge of myself, I wonder if we really believe in the relativity of behavior—professional protestations notwithstanding.

As social scientists have recently become increasingly self-aware of the roles both they and their disciplines play in their embeddedness in the social structure, they are increasingly unable to hide beneath the value-free myth of science. Increasingly they are confronted with greater self-knowledge, knowledge about why they study what they study, and the relationships between their work and other groups in society. As self awareness increases within criminology, we shall at least possess greater knowledge of what we are doing as we continue our work, greater knowledge of the implications of our research, and, I presume, a concomitant greater responsibility for our acts. But perhaps, just perhaps, our growing self-awareness will enable us, as men of good will and not simply as scientists, to grope for alternatives. And perhaps in our groping we shall find them.

But perhaps there is no alternative to the present emphasis in criminology. Perhaps we are faced with either disbanding or being handmaidens to the state.

REFERENCES

Becker, Howard S.: *Outsiders.* New York, The Free Press of Glencoe, 1963.

Chiricos, Theodore G., Jackson, Phillip D., and Waldo, Gordon P.· Inequality in the imposition of a criminal label, *Social Problems, 19*:553-572, 1972.

Costner, Herbert L.: Panel statement for the crime and delinquency section, SSSP *Newsletter*, 2:6-8, 1971.

Hall, Jerome: *Theft, Law and Society*, 2nd ed. Indianapolis, The Bobbs-Merrill Company, Inc., 1935, 1952.

Hindelang, Michael J.: The commitment of delinquents to their misdeeds: do delinquents drift? *Social Problems, 17*:502-509, 1970.

Hughes, Everett C.: Good people and dirty work. In Becker, Harold S. (Ed.): *The Other Side.* New York, The Free Press of Glencoe, 1964.

Ichheiser, Gustav: *Appearances and Realities.* San Francisco, Jossey-Bass, Inc., 1970.

Jeffery, C. Ray: The historical development of criminology. *J Crim Law, Criminol, Police Sci, 50*:647-666, 1959.

Johnson, Kenneth: *Mexican Democracy: A Critical Review.* Boston, Allyn and Bacon, 1971.

Lemert, Edwin M.: *Social Pathology.* New York, McGraw-Hill Book Co., 1951.

Liazos, Alexander: The poverty of the sociology of deviance: nuts, sluts, and perverts. *Social Problems, 20*:103-120, 1972.

Manning, Peter K.: Crime and the law as social problems. Mimeographed paper, 1970.

Quinney, Richard: *The Problem of Crime.* New York, Dodd, Mead and Company, 1970.

Radzinowicz, Leon: *A History of English Criminal Law and Its Administration from 1750.* New York, The Macmillan Co., 1948, 1957.

Schervish, Paul G.: Deviance as a political strategy: the trial of the Chicago 15. Paper delivered at the Twenty-First Annual Meeting of the Society for the Study of Social Problems, 1971.

Skolnick, Jerome: *The Politics of Protest.* New York, Bantam Books, 1968.

Sutherland, Edwin H. and Cressey, Donald R.: *Principles of Criminology,* 7th ed. Philadelphia, J. B. Lippincott, 1966.

Tilly, Charles: Collective violence in European perspective. In Graham, H. D. and Gurr, R.: *Violence in America: Historical and Comparative Perspectives: Report Submitted to the National Commission on the Causes and Prevention of Violence.* New York, Bantam Books, 1969.

Turk, Austin T.: Prospects for theories of criminal behavior. *J Crim Law, Criminol, Police Sci, 55*:454-461, 1964.

Vold, George B.: *Theoretical Criminology.* New York, Oxford University Press, 1958.

Walker, Daniel: *Rights in Conflict.* New York, Bantam Books, 1968.

Wheeler, Stanton (ed.): *Controlling Delinquents.* New York, John Wiley & Sons, Inc., 1968.

Wolfgang, Marvin E.: Criminology and the criminologist. *J Crim Law, Criminol, Police Sci, 54:* , 1963.

CHAPTER 3

DIFFERENTIAL DISTRIBUTION OF PEDAGOGIC RESPONSIBILITIES IN THE TRAINING OF HUMAN RESOURCES FOR CRIMINOLOGY: SOME THOUGHTS ON LEAA'S CENTERS OF EXCELLENCE PROGRAMS

GERHARD O. W. MUELLER, J.D., LL.M., DR.JUR.
(h.c.) (Uppsala)

Professor Mueller is director of the Criminal Law Education and Research Center, New York University School of Law, New York, New York. Professor Mueller is also a Professor of Law at New York University School of Law, is a past President of the American Society of Criminology and is presently Vice-President of the International Association of Penal Law.

COMMENCING WITH THE BUDGET year 1971-1972, the Law Enforcement Assistance Administration (LEAA) of the United States Department of Justice proposes to establish ten regional criminal justice "Centers of Excellence," largely to deal with the acute manpower shortage facing our profession. These are some first thoughts on the immensity of this undertaking, on priorities, and on proposed modes of proceeding.

THE NEW CRIMINAL JUSTICE SYSTEM AND ITS DEMANDS

It is fair to say that the American system of criminal justice today, including research and education in criminal justice, bears little relation to the system in existence a quarter century ago. Basically, in 1960, as in 1950 and in 1920, criminal law was the most badly neglected field in law in America, in practice as well as *in academia.*

Criminal law practice was in the hands of the least respected members of the profession, by rules which had changed little since the 1850's, according to constitutional standards that were not honored in practice, devoid of insights into the functioning and impact of the system.

While academic criminology existed, it was given virtually no chance of applying its precepts and insights on the functioning of the system, and its findings were relegated to the realm of theory. In the corrections part of the system—then referred to as penology—a seemingly unshakable belief in retribution and general and special deterrence barred practical entrance of a corrections-oriented approach.

In American universities the subject of criminal law was regarded as a *noli me tangere* by all "reputable" professors. Apart from a dozen or two exceptions, the subject of criminal law was assigned to teachers against their will, who quickly switched to more agreeable subjects as they advanced in seniority. Criminal law usually was the only required course within the area of criminal justice, and it was generally restricted to two semester hours. Criminal procedure, if offered at all, was optional in the third year, taken by few students, and dull in its coverage of 19th century forms of pleading. Criminologically oriented subjects were unknown at law schools. Ventures into the realm of real life or participation in the practice of criminal justice were unheard of.

Reform endeavors were not totally lacking, but they remained isolated instances without penetrating or large-scale effect. Examples thereof are the American Law Institute's Model Code of Criminal Procedure, the subsequent drafting of the Federal Rules of Criminal Procedure (late 1920's to 1940's), and the American Law Institute's Model Penal Code (1950's to early 1960's).

Public attention to problems of crime and delinquency were restricted to journalistic or sensationalist reports of capital crime and execution, gang-land criminality, and police corruption. Governmental planning and budgeting for reform was generally unknown.

The traveller to America who remembers this scene and who

returns to the scene of American crime and criminal justice today must be as startled by the changes as the Japanese army ser-
geant who hid out in the Guam jungles for thirty years and returned to Nippon in 1972.

What Is the Situation Today?

No social phenomenon is as widely and deeply discussed and
analyzed as crime in America. Hundreds of thousands of new
careers have opened up in criminal justice administration. Planning offices have sprung up like mushrooms at every level of
government—city, county, state and federal. The yearly expenditure of federal funds for research, education, and reform in
criminal justice reaches close to the two billion dollar mark.
With the recognition of "crime in the streets" as a paramount
American domestic problem, the Nation's foremost private research establishments have diverted their attention from military
logistics and space research to research and planning in criminal
justice. Crime is recognized as the fulcrum of America's racial
problems—the revolt of the disadvantaged who cannot reach the
posited ideals by legitimate means; it is also seen as a symptom of
the country's generation gap problems—the rebellion of youth
against overcome notions of propriety.

These changes have occurred, however, at a time when the
leaders of American criminological thinking, mostly from the
realm of sociology, had created the theoretical foundation,
premises, and methodology with which the new legal practitioners quickly analyzed the system and recognized it as totally in-
efficient, wasteful, and inhumane. Only a catalizer was needed
to bring criminological methodologists together with the young
core of criminal justice specialists from the law schools.

Governmental participation in the reform movement came in
the mid-sixties with the work of the President's Committee on
Law Enforcement and the Administration of Criminal Justice,
which released its magnificent report in 1967. The impact was
immense. Above all, the Law Enforcement Assistance Administration was created. This has become the government's largest
and most powerful—but by no means only—agency concerned

with research, planning, and reform in the area of criminal justice. It is also the distribution agency for vast federal resources devoted to that purpose.

With the coming into existence of this agency, large numbers of young criminologists of various disciplines left the area of theory and became the first generation of their discipline to practice what their preceding generations had taught them largely as a matter of theory.

Planning and reform in criminal justice, and more recently in the area of corrections as well, now requires close cooperation of personnel trained in various disciplines, predominantly law, sociology and social work, and now more frequently also in police science and administration. The spearhead of reform is, of course, the spin-off of theory into practice, in other words, action implementation. Even, and particularly, during their training process, students of law and other disciplines are actively involved in action-oriented projects, in so-called clinical programs, which combine planning, learning, service to the community and the system and its various "consumers" and ultimately reform. This then, in brief, is the story of the development of the "new system" of criminal justice education, research, reform, and action in America. These are also its basic ingredients.

It is too early to assess the system's impact, *in toto*. Indeed, for the time being, critics are justified in pointing out the shortcomings of the development: Public expenditure has increased vastly, yet the crime rate has seemingly increased significantly (or is it that we simply have learned to recognize its impact?). Victimization through crime seems at an all-time high. (Of course, twenty-five years ago there was no victimology.) The viciousness of our penal administration is widely recognized (before then, prisons were rarely regarded as fit objects for study).

There is a chance that, like so many political and other public phenomena in America, the interest in crime may simply be a passing fancy and may be discarded like a used toy in favor of a new priority, e.g. the protection of the environment. After all, do we not have thousands of unemployed scientists, who only yesterday were the heroes of America's program of space exploration?

Moreover, what permanent and lasting evidence of reform efforts to date is there? Have these reform efforts made any impact on the legal system? Has law codified the experience for systematic use?

What solid and scientifically acceptable experiences of the use of the criminal sanction are there before us, and have they been incorporated into penal codes which are really corresponding to scientific recognition as well as popular demand?

With all the clinical training that we are subjecting our students to, are we really providing for a permanent change of the system, or are we merely channelizing social action-oriented student energies away from revolution and into socially acceptable channels? Or are we even exploiting students as "cheap labor"? Is criminological research really capable of direct application, or are we spending vast research budgets simply to calm a guilty conscience which has tolerated decades of neglect and exploitation?

We need, above all, the answers to these questions:

1. Will the development continue in the same direction, will it change directions, will it stop or will it reverse itself?
2. Depending on the answer to (1), what is the system going to look like, ten, twenty, thirty years from now?
3. Depending on the answer to (2), what manpower needs will we have ten, twenty, thirty years from now?
4. Depending on the answer to (3), how can we train this manpower?
5. What social changes do we want to program into our training efforts?

It is believed that the education and training programs to be developed must provide a significant change from established curricula, leading toward integrated courses of study for the personnel preparing to enter, or already within, the criminal justice system. The combination of academic study with clinical service and field experience should provide a continuing closed-loop of input and feedback to enable the program to meet the demonstrable needs of the system.

Rationale of Educational Development

Over the last decade specialists in education, criminal justice, criminology and corrections have increasingly turned futurologists and have estimated the personnel needs of our criminal justice system. All these efforts, particularly that of the Joint Commission on Correctional Manpower and Training, have been unsuccessful for a variety of reasons:

(a) they assumed the system to be static;

(b) they assumed training techniques and efforts to be static;

(c) they largely assumed recruiting to be directed to the same personnel supplier groups; and

(d) they continued to think of the personnel of the future in terms of the rigid discipline demarcations of the past.

Not one educational establishment in North America has succeeded in establishing a coordinated university-wide program for the training of criminal justice specialists capable of maximal functioning in the system as it will appear in the predictable future.

This is not to say that the evolution of the criminal justice system did not have an educational impact. Per contra, never before have law enforcement and corrections personnel been as well trained as now, in academies established during the last few years. Colleges and junior colleges also have established law enforcement training programs all over the United States. On the professional level, departments of sociology and schools of law, medicine, public administration, and social work have intensified their efforts to produce persons capable of functioning in the system. Two or three American universities have established schools or departments of criminology on the postgraduate level, granting special masters and doctors degrees in criminology. A radically new nationally coordinated attack on the manpower problem is called for.

Targets

The targets or beneficiaries of the new proposed criminal justice manpower training programs are all parts of the criminal justice system, in particular:

1. Criminal Justice Planning Agencies (a totally new type of agency which did not exist just a few years ago), as well as reform groups
2. Law enforcement agencies
3. Court and other adjudicating agencies, including prosecution and defense
4. Correctional and after-care agencies and institutions
5. Diversionary agencies (especially employment and maintenance projects, therapeutic groups, etc.)
6. Related governmental establishments on all levels of government from municipal to United Nations governments
7. Research centers.

Currently, all of these agencies are only partially manned by personnel trained and educated for the job, with a consequent low efficiency rating, as attestable by any known means of inquiry, whether episodic or scientific. Unhappily, each of those agencies has been manned, traditionally, only by persons coming from one discipline, e.g. courts and adjudication agencies by lawyers, research establishments by sociologists, after-care agencies by social workers, etc.

Specific Aims

By institutionalizing guided change, we should break with the monoprofessional tradition by introducing trained personnel into the criminal justice system who have been educated with the requisite interdisciplinary sophistication. Only a university with the widest possible range of programs is capable of performing such a function.

It must be recognized that the criminal justice system of the present and the future has differential manpower needs, at different levels of education and sophistication, and that numerically these personnel needs decrease on the scale with increasing educational input:

Colleges and universities can fill only a portion—and perhaps the smaller portion—of these manpower needs. Personnel at the operative and service level can best be trained by academies and community college departments. Universities with strong gradu-

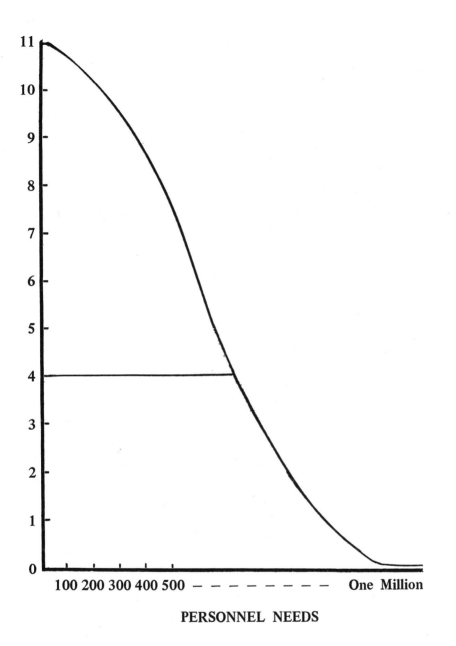

PERSONNEL NEEDS

Years of
University
training

Figure 1

ate schools, departments and divisions, and large research potential can more effectively train personnel on the managerial,
policy-making and professional level, including, however, leadership personnel on the operational level.

It is hoped that the Law Enforcement Assistance Administration's (LEAA) Centers of Excellence Program will result in the
creation of educational centers which are prepared to be operative at all levels of academic intake and output, from the first
year of college to the last post-doctoral training. But it is incum-
bent upon these centers to use cost-benefit analysis to assess their
priorities for the selection of those educational efforts which
have the largest possible impact on the system as a whole. Within
each institution this may require a concentration of effort at one
or several educational levels, but probably not all. Centrally-di-
rected university-wide assessments and coordination of efforts are
indicated.

Specifically, each center should:

1. assess its intake and output capacity in criminal justice and
   related areas of study;
2. design and develop new courses and curricula for these
   fields;
3. relate its training and research programs to the criminal
   justice systems' requirements; and
4. provide trained manpower at several levels of the criminal
   justice system.

PROPOSED EDUCATIONAL PROGRAM DEVELOPMENT FOR CRIMINAL JUSTICE CENTERS OF EXCELLENCE

Phase I—Assessment of Intake and Output Needs:
Program Solidification

As a first order of priority each interested educational institution should assess and reorder its intake and output capacity and
potential for education and training in criminal justice and related areas. The following model may serve as a point of departure:

(1) *Entrance* (student intake) into the institution's educational structure may occur at any one of many levels, from the

commencing first year of college to the postgraduate level of diplomate training in medicine, or the J.S.D. level in law:

An assessment is required as to
a. who enters the system
b. when
c. what for
d. why
e. with what expectations?

(2) *Exit* (personnel output) from the institution's educational structure likewise may occur at any one of many levels, from first year, e.g. extension programs, or after the second year, associate programs, to college completion, or the levels of the Masters or Doctors degrees, or after post-doctorate studies:

An assessment is required as to
a. who exists
b. why
c. to what
d. with what capacity
e. with what expectations?

These entrance and exit assessments require intense surveys of three controllable variables:

1. the supplier sectors of the population from which candidates for careers in criminal justice are being drawn;
2. the goals and personnel needs of the criminal justice system;
3. the educational structure and program content of the university units which connect points IA and IIB and thus constitute the center of the educational effort for excellence in criminal justice.

A university research, education, and service center in criminal justice has considerable influence over the control of all five of

Figure 2

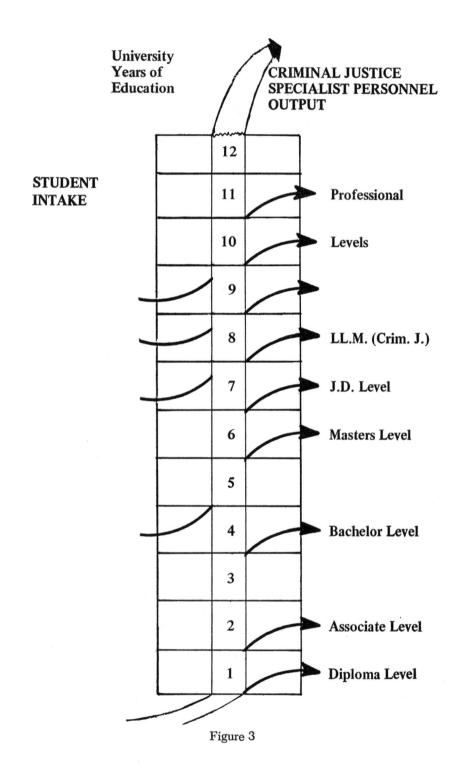

University
Years of
Education

CRIMINAL JUSTICE
SPECIALIST PERSONNEL
OUTPUT

STUDENT
INTAKE

12	
11	Professional
10	Levels
9	
8	LL.M. (Crim. J.)
7	J.D. Level
6	Masters Level
5	
4	Bachelor Level
3	
2	Associate Level
1	Diploma Level

Figure 3

these variables, particularly, however, over entrance, exit, and educational programs.

A graphic depiction of entrance→program→exit system can be examined below:

This graph, however, does not depict the variety of different educational programs which are in fact available to prepare a student for a career fully or partially devoted to criminal justice. At a given university, instead of one column "university years of education," there may be as many as ten or twelve. Some of these are shown on the following graph:

As demonstrated on the example of a law school, intake of students occurs at essentially two levels, and output, after completion of academic requirements, occurs at three.

At intake level one, college graduates, with or without life experience, with or without college specialization, are taken in, and lawyers are produced (output level 1). Through enrichment of the undergraduate studies, a law school becomes capable of producing specialists of a lower level of specialization for the performance of professional law functions within the criminal justice system.

At intake level two, lawyers with or without practical experience in the system, with or without law school specialization, are taken in and criminal justice specialists in law are produced (output level 2). Through considerable enlargement of a graduate law school program in the area of criminal justice studies, and the institutionalization of such degrees as Master of Laws in Criminal Justice (LL.M., Crim. J.), a law school is now capable of producing specialists of a high level of specialization for the performance of professional law functions within the criminal justice system.

An even higher level degree of skill and sophistication is acquired by those who continue their studies and complete their education with a Degree of Doctor of Juridical Science (J.S.D.), specializing in criminal justice.

Phase I of program development should consist of complete departmental surveys, focusing on:

1. student intake

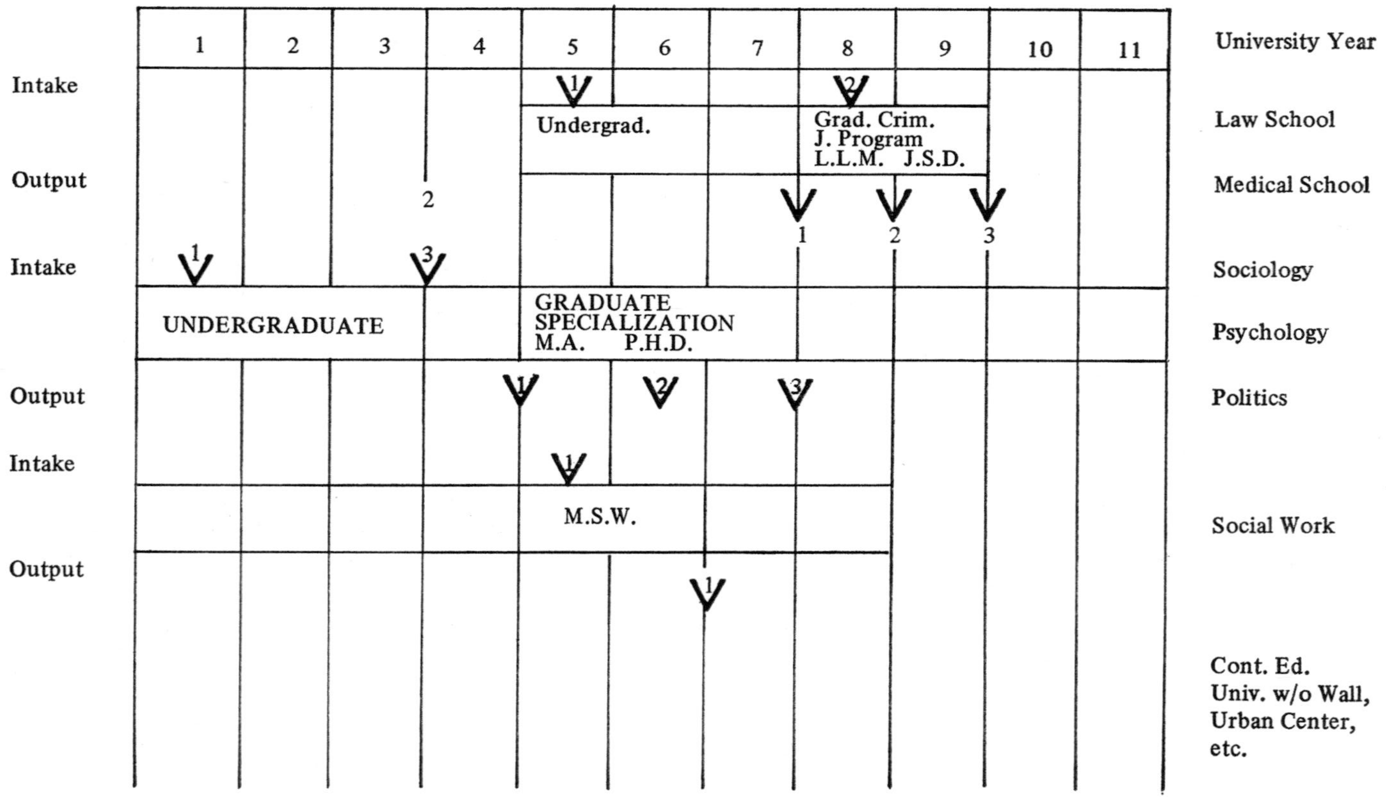

University Year

Law School

Medical School

Sociology

Psychology

Politics

Social Work

Cont. Ed.
Univ. w/o Wall,
Urban Center,
etc.

	1	2	3	4	5	6	7	8	9	10	11

Intake

Output

Intake

Output

Intake

Output

UNDERGRADUATE

Undergrad.

GRADUATE
SPECIALIZATION
M.A.   P.H.D.

Grad. Crim.
J. Program
L.L.M.   J.S.D.

M.S.W.

Figure 4

2. output
3. educational capacity and potential.

University-wide directed efforts must be undertaken to guide the intake, to control and steer the output, and to bring the university's educational capacity and potential to a maximum level of functioning. Intake guidance consists of attracting those potential students into the criminal justice system who can be expected to have the most beneficial impact upon the system.

Output control can be achieved through placement study and systematic placement efforts. Increase of academic capacity requires a prolonged effort, which must commence, but cannot end, during the first year of operation. In many, but not all departments, this will require an expansion of course offerings, addition of faculty, and increasing of the clinical outreach.

It is fully realized that not all participating departments of a university have a *primary* training interest, obligation or commitment in the sphere of criminal justice. For some, e.g. business administration and economics, the participatory role will extend only to program contributions.

On the other hand, for departments which are assuming primary training roles, the budget costs are likely to be distributed fairly evenly over all parts of the programs, whether graduate or undergraduate, on the basis of the old university experience maxim that instruction cost is related to an educational product composed of numbers of students on the one hand, and the standing in the academic echelon on the other, in inverse relationship to each other. In other words, one instructor can train perhaps 100 college juniors or 5 doctoral candidates. Policy decisions will have to be made, after the assessment of the university's present and future educational capacity, as to how to apply its pedagogical resources through planning; this will proceed along the lines of the most advanced cost-benefit and systems analysis thinking.

Above all, the first phase work should result in an effort to make each center's educational services available, nationwide, to young men and women who seek careers within the criminal justice system, regardless of discipline, with variable points of entry. A specific effort, however, must be made to attract those into the system who in the past have been excluded, that is to say, students from minority groups, women and, especially, ex-offenders.

Phase II—Interdisciplinary Efforts

The second phase in the development of Criminal Justice Centers of Excellence must focus on the enrichment of educational programs through interchangeability of courses within any or all of the participating departments. The theory behind this move is simple: The manpower needs of the system do not know discipline boundaries. A social worker within a correctional system must be familiar with the principles of psychological techniques. A sociologist employed in a criminal justice planning agency must be familiar with the laws and rules governing the criminal process. A correctional planner may require familiarity with business practices and cost-benefit thinking. A forensic psychiatrist must know the rules of substantive criminal law, and even a lowly corrections officer must be familiar with the total system. No one school, program, or discipline can afford to teach all the knowledge necessary for effective functioning within the system of criminal justice.

Consequently, each university must establish and effectuate a system for budget-conscious exchange of courses and seminars among all cooperating schools and departments. A student in any one of the schools is thus enabled to take those courses of any other school which are (1) geared to his level of sophistication and previous education and (2) of possible significance to a member of his professional expertise.

Interchangeability of courses is not the only means of achieving this end. Other means include the creation of courses, jointly taught by instructors of various disciplines, and special courses taught by instructors of one discipline within the program of another discipline.

Phase III—Joint Degree Programs and Specialist Certification

Criminologists have often debated the merit of the various new programs leading to a degree in what is thought to be the new discipline of criminology. A majority have rejected these models for a variety of reasons, the principal one being that despite claims to the contrary, criminology is not a unitary discipline but rather a composite discipline.

Students in any of the participating departments, whether graduate or undergraduate, would continue to strive toward completion of their degree requirements in their own discipline, e.g. social work, sociology, law, medicine, etc. But the graduate of the new-type program no longer will have taken courses solely in his own school or department. To the extent permissible by law or rules of accrediting agencies, he will have been permitted, encouraged, or required to take courses outside his department of discipline to render himself more universally educated but also more specialized for entry into the criminal justice system. A political science student may, for example, have taken not only his own department's required courses and courses with special emphasis on criminal justice related subjects within his department, he may also have taken a sociology course in statistical method, a law school course in criminal justice administration, and an urban center course in neighborhood decentralization, etc.

Each institution of higher learning must commit itself to the creation of a system of specialist certification. In cooperation with all participating departments, and perhaps in consultation with the American Society of Criminology, specialist requirements should be established which will entitle the graduate to receipt of a certificate as a criminal justice specialist in addition to his regular degree or diploma. This totally novel system will have the advantage of not weakening the degree requirements of all participating departments, while permitting departmental and interdisciplinary specialization within the broad reaches of criminal justice. This specialist certificate will be available at all levels of academic output, whether with a two year diploma, the college degree, or a Masters or a Doctors degree. The specialist certificate will state the degree which is simultaneously obtained and the major discipline of the graduate.

Conclusion

The proposed reorientation of programs and efforts for training criminal justice specialists avoids two ancient pitfalls: the creation of criminologists who are masters of no discipline, on the one hand, and the saturation of the profession with mono-professionals, on the other. On the professional level it envisages the criminological specialization of members of all disciplines whose expertise is required for the maximally efficient operation of the criminal justice system. It would leave undisturbed the special education of vocational members of the system in academics and special schools.

CHAPTER 4

THE NECESSARY CRIMINOLOGIST?

————————————— LESLIE T. WILKINS —————————————

Professor Wilkins teaches at the School of Criminal Justice, State University of New York, Albany, New York. He has been the recipient of the Sutherland Award for significant contributions to the field of criminology.

THE JUSTIFICATION for this paper is contained in a cable which stated something about my being adjudged a person who had made "significant contributions" to the field of criminology. I could not help pondering the terms of the Award: "Significant contributions." The word "significant" interested me. Years ago I used to consider myself a statistician, and some of my friends who did not know better concurred in this self-concept. I stayed with the field of statistics long enough to see the idea of "significance" challenged, and this concept which had held a central position in statistical theory become eroded, qualified, and modified. In the light of this experience I began to think what "significant contributions" I might have made to the field of criminology. However, before I had made much progress along these lines of introspection, a more serious question arose. Even supposing that some "significant contributions" had been made, what was the SIGNIFICANCE of their "significance"?

The statistical idea of "significance" was, and still is, closely associated with the idea of a DIFFERENCE. Had, then, anything I had done merited the right to be seen as "different"? Was the difference "significant"? If so, was that a good thing or a bad thing? What, in any event, was a "significant difference"? A DIFFERENCE is, I think, "significant" if it mades a *difference!* But it usually takes quite a time for information to accrue on that point.

If it is possible for me to dismiss the first doubts that I know anything, then, how do I know that I know? Is it a sufficient criterion of knowing that the scientific community agree that "it is a fact"? What, in any case, is a "fact"? Should we say, with some contemporary philosophers of science, that we can no longer speak of "facts" but only of "acts" or, perhaps, of "acts and reactions"?

There is a phenomenon recognized by psychologists (at least in theory) termed the cognitive bind. There is a tendency for ways of thinking to persist beyond their maximal utility. In the recollections and self-assessment which has been spurred by the honor conferred upon me, much of the thinking I have applied might also be applied to the field of criminology. You may yourselves decide whether this is a cognitive bind, but it seems to me that there are problems involved in the idea of significance or relevance, the concept of uncertainty and claims to knowledge; I am sure you will share with me my interest in the new and developing information theoretic models.

This is not a philosophical paper. Nonetheless I wish to do a little more word-spinning to propel me towards my topic. In the course of discussions, references have been made to "criminological science." If the idea of a criminological science has meaning, perhaps it might be inferred that there is little difficulty with the concept of criminology. What is criminology? What is a "science"? It is, of course, possible to take a phenomenological approach to these questions. Quite simply we could begin by noting that we all are here. Without further consideration of the idea of labelling, we may say that we have at least this one thing in common. But is that all? Supposing that I were to ask the reader if he sees himself as a "criminologist." Do we all share the self-concept of ourselves as criminologists? I rather doubt it. You might like to speculate with me as to what proportion of readers might respond to that question and how you, yourself, would respond. Would those who see themselves as criminologists differ in any major characteristics from those who do not? The outside world, however, sees the majority of us as criminologists, but to what extent would we agree with the definition by others? What kinds of experience do we claim, and how does this compare with the expertise we are expected to possess? I am sure that many of you have been placed in embarrassing positions when you were expected, as a criminologist, to have particular kinds of expertise which was not by any means concordant with your self-image. I am quite sure that if we were to proceed in our analysis in this manner, i.e. from the phenomenological viewpoint, we could run into some quite interesting and difficult problems.

We might, perhaps, move towards a taxonomy of knowledge in the field of criminology and, at the same time but independently, towards a typology of criminologists.

I am wandering into two different fields of thought; one is the idea of the self-image and its related product image. The other one is the idea of classification by kinds of information. It would be possible to develop the theme of THE NECESSARY CRIMINOLOGIST from either of these reference points. Right now, however, I am interested in a somewhat different approach to this question. Is there a body of knowledge which we might call "criminology"? Or would "criminal justice" be a better term? Does the terminology matter? In any event, how can we make any claims to knowledge? Do we need a collective of persons called "criminologists" or "criminal justicians" before we can lay claims to a body of knowledge? The Lockean idea of the community of scholars who give support to, and provide the criterion of verification for, our claims to knowledge may be somewhat circular.

Whether criminology is or is not a science seems to me to be hardly worth debating. Whether the investigations which are carried out in the field of reference utilize the scientific method would seem to be a much more important question and one upon which there is likely to be more agreement. I would not claim that investigations which utilize the "scientific method" are value free. Rather I would claim that the "scientific method" provides us with a means for uncoupling the investigator from the field of study to the greatest possible degree. I would claim that research is not a search for truth, but rather that it is the deployment of a strategy. Hence our considerations with regard to research methods involve questions of strategies and even of tactics. But I think there is an overriding finding which can be seen in criticisms of research methodology—no system can be effectively monitored by its own activities. In other words, there must be an *uncoupling* of the informational sensing devices from the system which generates the information by means of its activity. For this reason I welcome the new approaches to the obtaining of statistical data regarding crimes from studies of victims and by self-reports. I do so wholly or mainly because these methods provide a means for the collection of information which is not directly coupled into the system generating the activity to which the data relate. The latter conditions applied until very recently and to date only victim and self-report represent "uncoupled" information. But the mere collection of information is not an end in itself. We have to find ways for the recoupling of the information to the machinery of action. I think this may be one of the more important roles for the NECESSARY CRIMINOLOGIST. The criminologist is a person who can identify the means and strategies both for the uncoupling of the subsystems and for the recoupling of information to the control systems.

Perhaps I may now make some assumptions about what might have happened, if, in response to my earlier question to this audience, I had obtained information as to exactly how individual persons saw themselves. I suspect that some would say that they were psychologists, others sociologists, some lawyers, and I suspect there would have been a criminologist or two! I would think that almost every field of academic activity and discipline might claim at least one representative in our midst. We have a collective focus of interest and application. How closely should these disciplines be coupled together? Should we lose our individual identity in the collective consciousness of being "criminologists"? Is it necessary for a psychologist to cease to see himself as a psychologist when he becomes also a criminologist? Can I be a statistician and a criminologist too, please? I see no objection to bilingualism, far from it.

I said that I saw the problem of monitoring the criminal justice processes and the problem of engineering change in social control procedures as necessitating the uncoupling of information collection regarding the working of the machinery from the essential elements of that machinery itself. I said that this was one of the tasks for methodology and for a related strategy.

However, while stressing the need for uncoupling I want also to stress the need for recoupling. There is a term for this kind of thing in systems theory; we talk of an *interface.*

The NECESSARY CRIMINOLOGIST is, then, in my view, to function as an *interface:* coupling and uncoupling, separating conceptually and reintegrating conceptually, moving a problem from the field to the laboratory and back again as the situation and the state of knowledge demands and his information increases. There is a need for disciplines to be uncoupled, and there is a need to recouple disciplines in tasks which our humanity demands.

Ross Ashby, one of the greatest thinkers in the field of cybernetics to date, proposed a law which he terms the *Law of Requisite Variety.* Ashby himself states this in its simplest form as, "only variety can destroy variety." Of course there are elegant mathematical forms for this law. One of the simplest may be stated:

Let Vd be the variety of D (say, decisionmaker)

Vr the variety of R (say, response)

Vo the variety of outcomes

Then Vo cannot be less than the value Vd − Vr

or, Vo's minimum is Vd − Vr (Ashby, 1968).

I chose the NECESSARY CRIMINOLOGIST as a title because criminal justice has to do with regulatory functions in society, and regulatory functions are problems in cybernetics. An essential idea in *control* is the idea of *variety.* Whatever element is seen as needing to be controlled, this element is capable of generating variety: Variety demands variety for its control. The NECESSARY CRIMINOLOGIST must, therefore, have within his approach and philosophy the central idea of variety.

In the British Civil Service, in which I spent exactly twenty years, there is a policy which may be expressed in the form:

THE SPECIALIST SHOULD ALWAYS BE ON *TAP,*
NEVER ON *TOP*

Who then should be "on top"? Who is to control the controllers? I think that there is only one answer and a simple one to the ultimate question about control; the controllers must be controlled by the controlled! We have to find a way for providing a feed-back loop in such a form that this is possible. The information generated provides the means of control in the system to guide the controllers of that system. This is the task which should be engaging us at this time.

In the British Civil Service there was some kind of an approximation to this idea. The answer there to the question "who, if not the specialist, should be on top" was the GENTLEMAN AMATEUR. (The term includes women-gentlemen with due equality.) Both words are equally important—"gentleman" and "amateur." An amateur is not, of course, an ignoramous. An amateur is well learned (if not skilled) in many areas. He does not *identify* with any special area of expertise. But let me concentrate on the term, "gentlemen." Perhaps we could substitute the term "humanitarian" or "humanist" as being more appropriate in contemporary society. Thus, the "gentleman," while not a specialist, was informed and represented no faction, party, or interest.

When we look at the different disciplines concerned with problems relating to social control, we see professional identifications of varying kinds and intensities. When we meet as "criminologists" we should meet as "gentlemen." We should focus our expertise through the filter of humanitarian considerations. We should develop our functions as an *interface* and as agents for change. We need variety in social control, not conformity; we need to be able to utilize variety, not to seek to destroy it. Law enforcement should provide a climate in which variety can flourish. In action and also in research we should use variety and not merely regret its presence. We should do this in our research by studying not only the person who is defined as the criminal, and not only the person who is defined as the victim; we should study not only *persons*, but situations and decisions as well.

If I may steal, and then twist a phrase, I might say that the proper study for some criminologists should be criminologists.

REFERENCE

Ashby, W. Ross: Variety, constraint and the law of requisite variety. In Buckley, W. Aldine (Ed.): *Modern Systems Research for the Behavioral Scientist.* Chicago, 1968.

PART TWO

EDUCATION WITHIN THE CRIMINAL JUSTICE SYSTEM

CHAPTER 5

STAFF TRAINING AND DEVELOPMENT: THE TEACHING OF CRIMINOLOGY TO PERSONNEL WITHIN THE PENAL SYSTEM

——————— PAULA M. NEWBERG ———————

Professor Newberg is Assistant Professor of Law Enforcement and Corrections, Coordinator for Correction Programs, Public Service Institute, City Colleges of Chicago, Chicago, Illinois.

INTRODUCTION

TODAY, ALL ARE CONCERNED with the problem of law and order in our respective societies. This is not unique and has always been a dilemma for man: the problems of law and order, crime and punishment, and its control and correction.

It is the responsibility and problem of society to protect its members. One such means is by a judicial system and its processes. The Criminal Justice System has three broad components in the United States, as in most countries: the police system, the court system, and the system of corrections. They are separated in role and function, each with its destined tasks and its organizational components. But, the police, courts, and corrections are interrelated and are by no means independent; one can not function without the other. There is a true interdependency of one to the others.

Corrections and its apparatus is an integral part of the total judicial process, but it has been the most isolated part of the system in many ways. The correctional apparatus is physically isolated by walls, locks, and location. The personnel is more isolated from the other systems in its working relationships and in what it does with and to the persons committed to their systems. Society has often used the correctional apparatus to put away its problems and its disturbances: those that have failed society or that society has failed.

CORRECTIONS TODAY

Corrections today consists of scores of types and kinds of institutions, programs of the utmost diversity in approach, quality, philosophies, and regimes of control, from extreme leniency to the severest of confinement and harshness.

Corrections in America and throughout other countries is represented by many agencies and institutions, public and private, for the adult and juvenile, for the male and female. All are focused upon the correction of the behavior that has violated the laws of society. Contained and controlled by correction are varied types and kinds of offenders, representing offenses from a single truancy and minor infraction to mass murderers. The system is administered, controlled, supervised, and guarded by a wide range of personnel, ranging from educated and trained penologists to uneducated and ill-trained personnel whose main function is to turn a key or to shoot.

Society has become aware of the need for improved correctional programs as have the members and participants of the total judicial system. As we look at consistent and increasing crime rates, increased use of violence, the more frequent incidences of social disorders and disturbances, and the concern of the citizen for his personal safety and protection, public and political concern has been generated for law and order and the seeking of more effective solutions and answers on the combating and controlling of these problems. Such an example is the major crime control legislation of the 1960's—the first of its kind in American history.

Those directly concerned with the problems of crime and its control are questioning the effectiveness of the present correctional operation and system, with its fragmented information and divergent methods, philosophies and approaches (Valde, 1971). Within the United States, of the over 400,000 incarcerated, 95 percent will again re-enter society, and a majority of these will again be incarcerated for further violations (Valde, 1971). The more one is exposed to the correctional system, the greater the chances are that one will continue to reenter a life of crime, constantly being in and out of the correctional system (Lewin, 1968).

THE RATIONALE FOR THE UTILIZATION OF PERSONNEL WITH THE PENAL SYSTEM

One of the goals of correction is the prevention of additional crimes; in reality, however, this has not been accomplished. Authorities state that we must have more effective functioning of corrections. One positive means for the attainment of this objective is the acquisition and utilization of more information which can contribute to a better and more effective knowledge of corrections (Fox, 1968).

Here will be presented a frame of reference: pertinent knowledge and correctional practices which are essential to better equip personnel for more effective functioning within the correctional system.

Of the total number of personnel in corrections over one-half are engaged in custodial functions or classified as semiprofessional and nonprofessional with the American system (Fox, 1968).

It is now realized that there is an available resource and potential within these personnel as correctional officers. Means must be utilized to develop it. Presently, as there has been and as future predictions project, there are and will be serious personnel shortages in most fields of correction, and that the use of the semi- and non-professional can be utilized. But, they must be equipped with more training and knowledge, that is a necessity. The training of those in corrections has been limited in nature and scope. At times there has been none. For too long the majority of correctional staff, the correctional officer, has been neglected with regard to training and the utilization of potential. For a more effective correctional system, who has more contact and control with its charges than the keeper? It may be administration and directors that decide policies, orders, decisions, but they are initiated and carried out by the staff. It is the staff that has the frequent and daily contact with the contained population. The day-to-day operation is in their hands; the maintenance, functioning and control of that particular correctional apparatus is their domain. Tasks and decisions must be carried out by them, and often momentous decisions and actions must be decided. And yet, in most instances, the staff has not been adequately trained nor given the necessary tools of knowledge required. Other tools besides a key, badge, handcuffs, etc. are of necessity.

A certain scope of information regarding corrections must be transmitted to the worker to enhance his functioning and gain further insight into his work, his domain, and the institutional world. When the correctional officer acquires basic knowledge of his field and job, he realizes that he is not just a keeper and guard. He develops a greater understanding, a greater potential, and a more positive manner with fellow workers, staff administration, and charges. He can attain dignity and security; his job is more than guarding and securing. As a correctional worker, he has direction and purpose.

This group of better trained and more knowledgeable personnel demonstrates the enhanced effectiveness provided by their background:

1. The improvement of the capabilities of the personnel in the daily operation and maintenance of the institution.
2. Increased effectiveness of the personnel through realization of individual potential, resulting in great efficiency of the work force.
3. Aiding the personnel to recognize, understand, and handle problem situations that do occur within institutions and corrections.
4. To further aid personnel in the realization of greater job satisfaction through acquisition of information and training concerning work. Also the demonstration of occupational opportunities in correction.

The writer acknowledges that to develop an effective correctional staff, to maintain, operate, and achieve the organizational objective and goals of the correctional system, there must be several types of preservice, in-service, and on-going training programs for all ranges of personnel. This presentation is one such means, and includes the topics of knowledge that should be conveyed for the training and development of the involved personnel that in the past have received minimal attention.

PRESENTATION OF PERTINENT INFORMATION

The information that is to be taught and conveyed to the involved personnel group, enabling more effective functioning and greater role insight, is presented within the following major areas:

1. *An Overview of Corrections Today*

A topical look at trends, practices, programs. A review of more appropriate theories concerning crime and correction.

2. *Information Related to the Historical and Developmental Aspects of Criminology and Corrections*

A review of developmental theories and trends that have contributed to the present day situation of criminology and corrections are cited. Demonstrated are some "new" techniques and philosophies that are reflections of the past: how societal values and means have influenced the treatment and handling of crime and punishment up to the present.

3. *Issues Related to Types of Institution and Organizations*

It is of necessity that the personnel be aware of the varied type of institutions in terms of security, type of offender, short and long-term institutions, etc. An assessment is made of present types of institutions as to their effectiveness and their goal. Replacement is discussed in many areas as in funds, structure, administration.

4. *The World of the Institution*

A review and discussion of how theories of criminology and corrections explain the consequences of the institutional world. Attention is focused on aspects of socialization of both inmate and staff in this realm, and of whom and to what. Types of programs are examined and evaluated. Special problem areas within the institutional environment are delineated and discussed in terms of their management and the minimizing of them within the structure. Structural problems are examined that are so created by that particular environment.

5. *Alternative to Institutionalization*

It is imperative that the correctional worker realize his role within the totality of correction, and in presenting an overview of corrections this will enhance his perspective. Pre-post alternatives and programs of societal protection are reviewed and their merits and limitations.

6. *The Role of the Correctional Officer*

The development and changing role of those in corrections is examined. Emphasis is placed upon the officer as a "change agent," his realm of function is to the environment and its members, and the essentials necessary for his training and knowledge to enable him to fulfill the "new role" with its opening responsibility and challenge. The professionalism of corrections is discussed in terms of rationale and the means for attaining this new level.

Summary

Information and material highlighted in the presentation is a cumulative summary interpretation of a two year pilot program initiated for correctional officers at one of the largest penal systems within the Northern Hemisphere, and also from work with other national correctional systems and their respective authorities. Thus presented are only some of the concepts and information established by the program and those which would be pertinent to a panel discussion and to stimulate further communication on the conveying of knowledge to those within a penal system.

REFERENCES

Alexander, Myrle E.: *Jail Administration.* Springfield, Charles C Thomas, 1957.

Barnes, Harry E.: *New Horizons in Criminology.* New York, Printice-Hall, 1952.

Bennet, James V.: *Of Prisons and Justice: A Selection of the Writings of James V. Bennet.* Prepared for the subcommittee on National Penitentiaries of the committee of the judiciary United States Senate. Washington, U.S. Govt. Printing Office, 1963.

Campbell, James S., Sahid, Joseph R., and Strong, David P.: *Law and Order Reconsidered.* A staff report to the National Commission on the Causes and Prevention of Violence. Washington, U.S. Gov't Printing Office, 1969.

Clemmer, David: *The Prison Community*. New York, Reneteed, 1959.

Cloward, Richard, Cressey, Ronald R., Grosser, George H., McCleary, Richard, Ollin, Lloyd E., Sykes, Gresham M., and Messinger, Sheldon L.: *Theoretical Studies in Social Organization of the Prison*. New York, Social Science Research Council, 1960.

Committee on Personal Standards and Training: *Correction Officers Training Guide*. Washington, The American Correctional Association, 1969.

Conrad, John P.: *Crime and Its Correction*. Berkeley, University of California Press, 1967.

Conrad, John P. (Ed.): The future of correction. *The Annals*, 381:00-00, 1969.

Cressey, Donald R.: *The Prison: Studies in Institutional Organization and Change*. New York, Holt, Rinehart, Winston, 1961.

Fox, Vernon: *Guidelines for Correction Programs in Community and Junior Colleges*. Washington, American Association of Junior Colleges, 1968.

Goffman, Erving: *Asylum*. Garden City, Doubleday & Co., 1961.

Hazelbrigg, Lawrence: *Prison Within Society: A Reader in Penology*. Garden City, Doubleday & Co., 1971.

Jeffery, C. Ray: *Crime Prevention Through Environmental Design*. New York, Russell Sage Publications, 1968.

Johnson, Elmer: *Crime Correction and Society*. Homewood, Dorsey Press, 1968.

——: Personal problem of corrections and the potential contributions of the university. In *Report Center for the Study of Crime, Delinquence, Corrections*. Carbondale, Southern Illinois University, 1968.

Lewin, Stephen: *Crime and Its Prevention*. New York, H. W. Wilson and Co., 1968.

Mann, W. E.: *Society Behind Bars: A Sociological Scrutiny of Guelph Reformatory*. Toronto, Social Sciences Publishers, 1967.

Menton, Robert J.: *Inside—Prison American Style*. New York, Random House, 1971.

Schrag, Clarence: *Crime and Justice: American Style*. Rockville, National Institute of Mental Health, .

Sparks, Richard: *Key Issues in Criminology*. London, World University Library, 1970.

Tannenbaum, Frank: *Crime and the Community*. New York, Columbia University Press, 1963.

Tappan, Paul V.: *Crime, Justice, and Correction*. New York, McGraw-Hill, 1960.

United States President's Commission on Law Enforcement and the Administration of Justice: *Task Force Report: The Challenge of Crime in a Free Society*. Washington, U.S. Gov't Printing Office, 1967.

CHAPTER 6

HIGHER EDUCATION FOR CRIMINAL JUSTICE CAREERS

—————— RICHARD A. MYREN ——————

Professor Myren is Dean of the School of Criminal Justice, State University of New York at Albany, Albany, New York.

CRIMINAL JUSTICE PROGRAMS are now well established components of higher educational institutions in the United States at all levels, offering the Associate in Arts degree in the community colleges, the baccalaureate in the four-year colleges, and the doctorate in the universities (Myren, 1970). Although relatively new, these programs have found their identity as integrated interdisciplinary sequences of scholarly research and teaching in the behavioral and social sciences (defined to include law and public administration) focused on the social problem of crime. As such, they are neither disciplinary nor professional but rather exemplars to the new kind of higher education effort in the behavioral and social sciences recommended by the BASS report (National Academy of Sciences and Social Science Research Council, 1969).

As a field of study in higher education, criminal justice is broader in its substance and approach than traditional criminology, long recognized as a subfield of sociology. It also encompasses but is, at the same time, broader than crime-related sequences familiar to us as elements of the curricula of law schools, political science and public administration departments, and programs in clinical psychology. It must concern itself with at least five areas: the nature of crime and its relationship to other kinds of deviance as well as to conformity; the nature of society's reaction to crime, both historically and in the present, which requires exploration of all past and current crime control theories, informal as well as formal; the organization and operation of criminal justice systems as one common formal social control mechanism; the nature of personal, organizational, and institutional change along with the skills and strategies for achieving that change; and design of the research so badly needed to expand our very meager fund of knowledge about crime, together with the methodologies most apt for implementation of those designs in a generally inhospitable research setting.

Integration of the variety of insights and approaches of the traditional behavioral and social sciences into a concentrated sequence dealing with the social problem of crime is no easy task. Well rounded professors, specially educated for this field, have not been generally available; they are, however, beginning to emerge from the less than handful of strong graduate programs created or recreated in the late sixties. Meanwhile, criminal justice programs require interdisciplinary faculties functioning as a separate academic unit. Neither simple joint appointments nor complex consortium arrangements will serve. Faculty development is fully as important as student development. This requires a faculty immersed in the process: housed in one location so that corridor conferences, lunch and coffee-break conversations, as well as more formal office discussions and consultations can conveniently occur; team teaching engaged in by professors from different disciplines as a formal interchange of insights and approaches; team work in committee assignments aimed at further program definition and development; and circulation of proposed article and book chapter drafts for comment by colleagues. This kind of immersion in a joint effort simply cannot and does not occur with more diffuse administrative structures. A separate department, school, or college is required.

This does not mean that there should not be related offerings in the basic discipline departments and professional schools. These are necessary complements, tied more closely to the narrower purposes of the disciplinary or professional program as necessary elements in those offerings. Indeed, such sequences are more apt to come into being and be of higher quality on a campus that has a strong criminal justice unit than on one without.

That unit, with its highly qualified and dedicated interdisciplinary faculty will serve as a source of strength for those professors in other units who wish to teach about and do research on crime problems from a disciplinary or professional perspective. Without the substantive support of a criminal justice faculty, such professors frequently have no one to talk to about their interest, a factor that sometimes causes abandonment of crime-related research and teaching.

Specialized programs are also needed in higher education to produce the manpower needed to staff the criminal justice system. Each year thousands of young men and women in the United States make commitments to careers they will follow for the rest of their lives. Despite the national attention that has been focused on crime by three successive Presidential Commissions during the decade that has just come to a close, very little has been done about building a criminal justice career system to attract these commitments. Establishment of such a system, that year after year rivals law, medicine, education, and the ministry in persuading well educated young people to devote their lives to work on crime problems, is one of the great needs of the criminal justice system in the United States today.

The need is for manpower of all types: operational, research, and teaching. It seems anomalous for scholars capable of and interested in working on crime problems to be devising sophisticated research designs and methodological techniques without concern for building a criminal justice system structure in which to do the research and without concern for developing a group of criminal justice system careerists capable of utilizing the research results.

This paper sketches the broad outlines of the kind of criminal justice career system that is needed and discusses the parallel program in higher education required to staff that system (Myren, 1970b).

NATURE OF THE CRIMINAL JUSTICE CAREER SYSTEM

What is needed is a criminal justice career system that will provide general managers for the fifty-odd systems of the United States today. A distinction must be drawn between system careerists who are wide-ranging generalists and employees who may be very narrow specialists or technicians needed in specific operations. The latter will be employed by the system as are those with similar skills elsewhere in the community. Such persons may range from elevator operators and automobile mechanics to attorneys and surgeons. What differentiates them from the career generalist is their functioning as specialists in a role defined as necessary by others, a policy decision in which they did not participate. Nor do they participate in other policy making. Such a specialist position might be held while preparing for a general career system position, but would not itself be one.

A true criminal justice career system will provide for free lateral and promotional transfer from positions in one agency to those in others. It will build system loyalties with the system goal always in mind. Concentration while in any given agency position will be on how that position and that agency can best contribute to achievement of the system goal.

Such a criminal justice career system will offer possibility of employment not only in a single criminal justice agency but in all of them. A typical career employee of the system will spend time in several if not all of the component agencies: police, courts, probation, correctional institutions, parole, and the various specialized agencies such as New York's Narcotic Addiction Control Commission. Only after such a diversified work experience in the first twenty or twenty-five years of his career will he be expected to settle into a particular component agency in a leadership role.

This vision of a criminal justice career system is based on the assumption that there will be general recognition and acceptance in the United States of the fact that it is the criminal justice system, and not single component agencies of that system, that has been given the task of controlling crime by our society. None of the individual criminal justice agencies has a separate identifiable goal, not the police nor prosecutors, not criminal court judges nor correctional officials. Only the criminal justice system as a system has been given the social goal of containment of crime. Much of the ineffectiveness of current government efforts stems from failure to realize this simple fact. Our criminal justice system has been so fragmented that component agencies exist in a state of warfare rather than cooperation among themselves. This results in large part from narrow-minded educational preparation of police, lawyers, social workers, and other social scientists employed in the system, the products of which go into even more narrowing careers spent entirely in a single agency.

A wide range of career lines will be open to talented young persons who cast their lot with the criminal justice career system here proposed. Among the specific positions available will be operational jobs at all levels in all agencies, many of which are quite similar in nature. A second type will be staff-liaison advisory positions with middle and top level officials in all three branches of government who have frequent and continuous contact with criminal justice agencies. A third kind of position will be in the in-house research units of the agencies—units that need new research talent desperately. A fourth type of position will be with the planning agencies beginning to turn their attention to crime problems at the federal, state, and local levels.

Outside the criminal justice system proper, it will also be possible for careerists who so desire to mix governmental positions with periods of research and teaching in crime-related programs in higher education, or, indeed, to spend their entire career in a college or university setting. Such sabbaticals or more extended periods of service will similarly be possible with careerist professional organizations and with private social and welfare agencies that deal with the same persons who become involved with criminal justice process.

Achievement of this new criminal justice career system will require built-in career ladders. It must be possible for young men and women who cannot afford or who for some reason are not motivated to seek a complete, sophisticated, pre-service education to the graduate level to obtain jobs in the system and then move upward to more responsible positions on the basis of in-service education and training, coupled with experience in the system. At the same time, it must be made possible for those who do obtain graduate level preservice education that includes experience in a research setting to move directly into middle and upper level career positions of responsibility throughout the system.

NATURE OF THE PARALLEL EDUCATIONAL SYSTEM REQUIRED

To make feasible the criminal justice career system here envisaged will require a parallel preparation system in higher education that will begin at the first year of college and provide a continuous learning, doing, teaching process throughout the contributing life of the criminal justice careerist. Every component of the educational experience will be as general as possible in recognition of the fact that crime has a social setting. In all aspects of the educational effort a balance must be maintained between acquisition of communication and other social skills: acquisition of that knowledge of individuals and society that leads to social and self-understanding, and acquisition of specific knowledge of crime as a personal and social phenomenon and of society's reaction to crime, past and present. This includes an intimate knowledge of the place of a criminal justice system as one social control mechanism among many, and of the current functioning of such systems.

Today's higher educational system has the flexibility necessary to provide this parallel educational ladder in its community colleges, four-year colleges, and universities. Those young persons who have the financial and motivational resources for postponement of profitable employment can obtain a bachelor's degree followed by an M.A. and even a Ph.D. in Criminal Justice. To be most fruitful, these undergraduate and graduate programs must have experiential components, preferably in a research setting.

Those persons seeking criminal justice careers who cannot commit themselves to an initial seven-year stint in higher education must be able to mix their educational experience with productive employment in the system. The sequence might be two years of college work, a period of employment in the system, completion of the baccalaureate, employment in the system, completion of a master degree, employment in the system, and, finally, completion of a doctorate. Educational leave on full pay and allowances must be made available for the educational periods in this sequence. Or there might be a continuous mix of part-time employment and part-time education as a planned career progression. These mixtures of employment and formal education require changes in attitude on the part of both the agency components of the criminal justice system and the various elements of higher education.

Assuming that a young person has made the decision to dedicate his life to work on crime problems and that he can and is willing to spend from four to eight years preparing for his career in some kind of higher education program, what are the alternatives open to him?

One route is to get a traditional baccalaureate in humanities or the social sciences and then do graduate work in a traditional professional field, usually law, social work, or public administration. Such an education has the advantage of opening up a wide range of employment opportunities should interest in the criminal justice system flag, should a suitable opportunity in that system not be available at job hunting time, or should the reality of work in the system prove to be, after a few months of employment, more than the individual can take.

Despite these obvious advantages to the individual, this kind of educational preparation is not the best for an eventual policy making role. It does not give the young person any particular insight into the difficult policy questions facing the system. It can prepare individuals to be system employees, but not system managers, system careerists. It is true that persons so prepared can earn system insight through experience and thus become career generalists, but this school of hard knocks is a difficult route fraught with hazards. All too frequently one so prepared becomes lodged in a single agency and never does obtain a view of the system as a system with a system goal. This is the lesson of the past.

Higher education also has had specialized programs leading to criminal justice *agency* careers for some time. These programs have developed for the two ends of the system: police and corrections. Development of the police programs is well documented; a similar history of academic programs in corrections is yet to be written. There remains an impression, however, that the police programs came earlier, and it is certainly true today that there are more of them of greater variety than of corrections programs. It is also largely from the police oriented programs, not from the correction oriented, that we have developed the needed system oriented programs for the future.

Despite the considerable number of such programs now in existence, neither the police nor the correction type ever really made it in the academic world. Existing largely in state supported institutions, they have never been held to the academic standards of other programs in higher education. They have been staffed by marginal social scientists and lawyers or by persons retired from some criminal justice agency whose life energy and talent was largely burned out in that first career. They have attracted students who, on the whole, could not make it in more traditional fields. As a result, these programs have been characterized by unimaginative curricula and teaching designed to perpetuate agency practices of the past. The programs, their students, and their faculties have been at the bottom of the academic pecking order. They have taken in a parasitic way from the programs of the main body of the college or university of which they were a part but made no return contribution. Isolated from the main stream of college life, they have been tolerated by the general faculty and administration as relatively cheap community service, that seemed to aid in loosening the purse strings of the legislative body from which funding came. The graduates of these programs have been narrowly agency oriented and have probably contributed to a more sophisticated solidification of criminal justice system fragmentation than existed prior to their availability.

To be more specific, resistance to police and corrections programs in our colleges and universities has resulted from a number of definite, identifiable factors. Perhaps the most basic has been their failure to attract academically qualified instructors. Among the general social science disciplines, work on crime problems has never been a high prestige specialization. This may have been true because the potential consumers of new knowledge and graduating students were a low prestige group, criminal justice practitioners. Little money was available to support research. Dealing as it does with the seamy side of society, the speciality has not been inherently attractive when compared with other possibilities. Whatever the reason, those few scholars in each of the basic disciplines who chose to work on crime problems were usually the lowest in status among that peer group.

And the better established the discipline, the more certain this has been. It is probably least true in sociology, which itself until the very recent past has been low in status. During sociology's fight for an established place, criminology fared better than crime-related specialization in other disciplines.

For all of these reasons, there were few crime specialists among academic social and behavioral scientists available to staff police and corrections programs. Those who did exist did not wish to jeopardize further their already precarious professional positions through formal full-time affiliation with an "applied," problem-oriented program. This meant that the new police and correction sequences were staffed largely with retired practitioners.

Such a staffing profile produced a trade school approach in which students were taught how their professors had faced career problems during their experience in a specific agency. Because the professors had neither training nor experience in research and no tradition of asking meaningful questions, this initial orientation did not soon get challenged. The mold was frozen for many years, a trade school mold. Because the programs were essentially nonacademic although housed in an academic setting, because their faculty members as second careerists did not share academic traditions, and because the programs took from the college but gave nothing in return, an isolation from general college life developed that was almost universal. Another factor reinforcing that isolation was that most of the instructors in the police and corrections program were political conservatives while academic faculties generally are politically liberal, making the crime-related faculty a right-of-center island in a left-of-center sea.

Some doubtless will disagree with this analysis of why police and correction programs in colleges and universities were resisted and isolated by academia, but few will deny that this in fact was generally the case from inception at about World War I until the very recent past.

As with all generalizations, there have been exceptions to the above description in terms both of individual instructors and programs. Some academically well prepared professors did join these faculties for one reason or another, and some instructors recruited from the ranks of practitioners proved to have both talent and imagination. Over the past fifteen years, the status quo *has* been challenged, and definite change trends *have* emerged. New programs *have been* and *are* being established that *do* focus, not on preparation for service in a single agency, but on understanding the criminal justice system as a system, a prerequisite in the education of a criminal justice system generalist. Establishment of this broader objective has succeeded in creating an academically viable field.

Conclusion

Criminal Justice programs that do meet traditional academic standards of excellence now exist at each level of higher education: in two- and four-year colleges and in graduate schools. Prototypes have been established, and newly created sequences more and more follow their lead. Most of the older programs, seeing the handwriting on the wall, are converting to the new model. On the whole, there is reason to believe that higher education is more prepared to educate talented young persons for a new style criminal justice career system than are the component agencies to reorganize themselves on a cooperative basis into a true criminal justice system.

REFERENCES

Myren, Richard A.: Building a criminal justice career tradition. Eighth Annual Conference Proceedings of the International Association of Police Professors, February, 1970.

———: *Education in Criminal Justice.* Sacramento, Coordinating Council for Higher Education in California, 1970.

National Academy of Sciences and Social Science Research Council: *The Behavioral and Social Sciences: Outlook and Needs.* Englewood Cliffs, Prentice-Hall, 1969.

APPRENTICESHIPS IN CRIMINOLOGY: THE INTEGRATION OF THEORY AND PRACTICE THROUGH INTERNSHIPS IN THE CRIMINAL JUSTICE SYSTEM

——— Dr. George L. Kirkham and Walter G. Turner ———

Professors Kirkham and Turner are members of the Department of Criminology, Florida State University, Tallahassee, Florida.

CRIMINOLOGISTS HAVE DISPLAYED considerable zeal in recent years directed toward the end of securing respectability for their fledgling discipline in the scientific community. This effort to win the interdisciplinary respect of scientific peers has perhaps been most evident in the manner in which criminologists themselves have defined their field. Researchers and teachers of criminology alike have tended to adopt definitions of their discipline which simultaneously emphasize its "pure" scientific pursuit of knowledge and relative lack of concern for the practical applicability of such knowledge.

The reluctance of most criminologists to risk any contaminative connection of their discipline with the realm of applied knowledge for fear of diminishing its scientific importance is apparent, e.g. in Sellin's definition of criminology: "The term criminology should be used to designate only the body of scientific knowledge and the deliberate pursuit of such knowledge. What the technical use of knowledge in the treatment and prevention of crime might be called, I leave of the imagination of the reader" (Sellin, 1938).

The majority of scientific criminologists reject the labeling of police officers, correctional workers, probation personnel, and other criminal justice practitioners as "applied criminologists" (Wolfgang, 1963). Beyond this, they appear relatively unconcerned about the ability of such individuals to apply the findings of scientific criminology to the analysis of systems and problems in their respective fields.

The authors are of the opinion that the contemporary tendency to equate criminology with pure science, and the resultant distancing of criminological scientists from exposure to the practical referents of their knowledge, has had unfortunate consequences for the education of both criminal justice practitioners and those who plan teaching and research careers in the field.

The concern of some criminologists with preserving inviolate the purity of their science has become transmuted into a philosophy under which criminology education has become little more than hollow rhetoric, a set of theories and ideals hurled from lecterns without much regard to either their comprehensibility or relevance to current realities.

Criminology professors are often heard to complain that both graduate and undergraduate students in the field manifest relatively little understanding of the body of knowledge to which they have been exposed in the educational process. For their part, students retort that what they have learned does not seem relevant or applicable to the analysis of the practical criminal justice problems and systems which they confront upon leaving the university setting. We believe that such sentiments are symptomatic of deficiencies in the character of contemporary criminology education.

A great many educators will react with unmitigated horror to the suggestion that a criminology education should involve some form of laboratory exposure to the practical referents of criminological knowledge. To perhaps the majority of criminology educators, the notion of "internships" suggests an unequivocal step backward for their profession—the transformation of criminology as a burgeoning scientific enterprise into some kind of preservice training program geared to turning out criminal justice practitioners. Internships are viewed by many in the field as the harbinger of a progressive infestation of legitimate curricula with "nuts and bolts" (Roebuck and Zalhart), courses to the point where nothing resembling a science of criminology is any longer taught.

The Value of Internships in Criminology Education

If one accepts the prevailing definition of criminology as ". . . a body of scientific knowledge about crime" (Wolfgang, 1963), the educational question arises as to just how this body of knowledge is best communicated. We may, therefore, meaningfully seek to identify optimum pedagogical techniques for the transmission of scientific knowledge concerning crime and criminals.

Many criminologists appear to feel that didactic lectures and related assigned readings constitute in themselves a sufficient basis for meaningful criminology education. However, as the majority of students will become practitioners, the authors take serious exception with such a view and regard criminology internships as an integral part of the educational process in our field.

To be sure, a great deal of knowledge is taught effectively in colleges and universities simply on the basis of formal instruction and assigned reading alone. It will here be suggested in this regard, however, that criminology educators are in quite a different position than for example professors of geography or economics. The interdisciplinary body of knowledge which presently constitutes criminology has a great many referents which are quite difficult for students to fully understand solely on the basis of formal instruction and solitary study. Ignorance on such subjects as offender characteristics and criminal justice processes is a component in the minds of many students by the existence of pervasively held stereotypes disseminated by the mass media.

Many students evince the same level of naiveté about crime and criminals after college that characterized their thinking prior to being exposed to a formal body of criminological knowledge. The multiplicity of concepts and theories which are presented in criminology lectures and texts fall upon the deaf ears of students who perceive such knowledge as largely abstract and unrelated to anything in the real world—the world of criminal justice practitioners.

No one would seriously suggest that the education of medical students should depend entirely on thousands of hours of lecture on the functioning and structure of the human body. Even the best of students would find it difficult to relate abstract knowledge to physiological reality in the absence of well-structured laboratory opportunities to minutely observe the latter. A meaningful medical education is recognized by all as necessarily having an experimental dimension to it. The authors wish to argue that, if it is to be comparably effective in preparing criminal justice careerists, criminology education must likewise include a corresponding "laboratory" dimension; students should have an opportunity to examine criminological knowledge against the backdrop of its practical referents—different kinds of offenders and forms of crime, criminal justice structures and processes, and the like. The opportunity to examine ideas in their referential context is simply a superior educational technique to the abstract transmission of knowledge per se.

As an illustration of the superiority of combined instructional-laboratory techniques in the field of criminology, let us consider an attempt to communicate to undergraduate students the applicability of "labeling theory" (Lemert, 1951) to an understanding of differential selection of offenders in the reality functioning of the criminal justice process. Students who have had the opportunity as criminology interns to ride in patrol cars and actually watch the police react to juveniles on the basis of "deference, demeanor, and appearance" (Pilivan and Briar, 1968) are apt to perceive the concept of "labeling" as a more meaningful and relevant one than those whose knowledge of the subject is limited to lecture and study material. Similarly, lecture and reading material on the prison social system is appreciably more significant to the student who has been afforded a laboratory opportunity to view a correctional facility as a total institution and actually observe the myriad norms and structures of prison life (Irvin, 1972).

The authors are of the view that the purpose of formal criminology education is twofold: (1) to transmit a body of scientific knowledge concerning crime; and (2) to develop in criminology students a capacity to critically apply such knowledge to an analysis of its practical referents. We do not believe that criminology can or should neglect the matter of its applicability as a dimension of scientific knowledge, and are in agreement with Johnson's view that "criminology has two interdependent branches, science and practice" (Johnson, 1968). For any science to ignore or divorce itself from the existential realities on which its concepts and theories are based is to invite stagnation and atrophy. Crime, delinquency, the criminal justice process are all dynamic phenomena which change rapidly; such changes must be recognized by both scientists and practitioners alike who have the ability to make appropriate modifications in concepts, theories, structures, and applications.

It matters little whether the recipient of formal criminology education plans to become a scientist or probation officer; both must have the ability to relate abstract criminological knowledge to individual and sociopolitical situations. For the criminal justice practitioner, such a capacity facilitates quite practical decision-making processes. The same ability is also essential to the criminological scientist who would engage in relevant teaching and research activities. A criminology education should enable both practitioner and scientist to extrapolate from the abstract realm of criminological knowledge and utilize this data in the analysis of tangible problems and systems. Thus conceived, criminology education is much more than a mindless process which grinds out a mass of data and theory without much regard to its relevance or applicability to reality or use.

What Is a Criminology Internship?

In attempting to define the nature of a criminology internship and differentiate it from the educational intern's "student teaching" or the "field placement" programs which abound in schools of social work, it may prove instructive to begin by stating what an internship *is not*. Criminology internships are not intended to in any way represent a means for providing prepractitioner students with job-specific skills or training in a particular criminal justice vocational area, though a certain degree of familiarity with such tasks and skills may be acquired as an incidental by-product of the intern program.

As the expression will be employed in this paper, a criminology internship is a highly structured "laboratory" experience which is intended to complement formal instruction and study in the discipline of criminology. It accomplishes this purpose by exposing students, under close academic supervision, to various practical referents of criminological knowledge. Above all, a criminology internship seeks to develop in students an ability to relate abstract criminological knowledge to the reality of crime and the various social and political processes and structures which surround it. It is, therefore, an educational—not a training—process.

How a Criminology Internship Operates

The educational significance of criminology internships may perhaps best be grasped by examining the structure and operation of one such program. The Department of Criminology at The Florida State University, Tallahassee, Florida, has had an internship program as an integral part of its undergraduate curriculum structure for over ten years. More than one hundred criminal justice agencies provide the "laboratory" settings in which the undergraduate student will spend one academic quarter in an attempt to achieve the difficult integration of knowledge and reality.

As the program is presently structured, interns-to-be usually select a general field of interest, i.e. police services, adjudication or habilitation, and a specific agency during their junior year and experience placement during the senior year. Prior to actually interning, students select, in consultation with their faculty advisor or the faculty internship coordinator, an area of criminological knowledge which particularly interests them. Once a concept, theory, or subject area has been decided upon, the student initiates an exhaustive study of relevant literature in advance of the coming internship. This is, of course, a relatively familiar process for students who have in most cases prepared a great many term papers by this stage in their academic careers. Here, however, the similarity with conventional academic assignments ends.

Having once examined all relevent literature on a topic, e.g.

the prison subculture, violent offenders, or the authoritarian personality, the student is prepared to carry this academic lens into a context where he can actually observe the individuals and processes to which it is relevant.

The student who is placed in a correctional, court, or law enforcement environment soon discovers that he must develop critical faculties of observation and awareness, as he confronts the formidable task of producing an internship paper in which abstract criminological knowledge must be related to the idiosyncratic details of his particular field experience. It is further expected that his review of the literature and internship experience will together enable him to critically discuss the views of various notables on the subject in question, and contrast them with his own views based on his internship experience. As the student intern grapples with the task of relating the abstract to the concrete, he receives assistance from practitioner and scientist alike: An agency supervisor is designated and represents an immediate practitioner resource, while regular weekly communications are maintained with the faculty intern coordinator who aids the student in the development of his project paper.

It can readily be seen that the internship experience represents a timely catalyst in the criminology student's educational career. It has been our observation that, whether a student goes on to become a criminal justice practitioner, as the majority do, or criminological scientist, he returns to the classroom after his internship with greatly enhanced interest in his field of study and a new found ability to relate abstract knowledge to its practical referents.

Other Advantages of Criminology Internships

It is possible to discuss several other benefits which accrue from the operation of criminology internship programs beyond the manifest one of providing students with a mechanism for relating knowledge to experience. Not the least of these is the establishment of a system of reciprocal communication and exchange of ideas between criminal justice practitioners and their agencies and criminological scientists and their institutions.

If one of the goals of criminology is, as Johnson suggests, ". . . to pass on to practitioners the fruits of the criminological sciences" (Johnson, 1968), internships represent an important vehicle for accomplishing this end. The constant influx of student interns, armed with the very latest in theoretical knowledge and research findings, provide criminal justice practitioners who receive and supervise them new insights which may be incorporated or applied to the analysis of contemporary criminal justice systems and problems.

Student internships also provide a major denouement to criminology researchers and educators by keeping them constantly abreast of dynamic changes in the working criminal justice system. It is, of course, essential that scientists in the field of criminology be constantly apprised of new developments in their areas of expertise and interest, in order to modify concepts and theories, and to generate new research activity. The continuous return of students to the classroom—fresh from internship experiences in police departments, probation-parole agencies, and other settings—provides professors of criminology with a mechanism for becoming aware of current developments in the criminal justice field. As a teaching criminologist, the senior author has more than once had what he believed to be the very latest information on a subject, or the applicability of some theoretical concept to a particular setting, challenged by a post-internship student who was possessed of more current and experientially derived knowledge on the point in question.

The Unrealized Potential of Criminology Internships

If criminology internships hold significant educational value for students, why might they not also be utilized by scientists who wish to expand their own experiential familiarity with particular subjects and generate new ideas for future study?

A number of criminologists are seriously handicapped in their effectiveness as teachers and researchers because of this lack of experiential familiarity with subject areas in which they have considerable formal knowledge. One may read at great length about police-minority group relations or custody-treatment conflicts in prisons and still have no real "feel for" either subject because he has never talked to a ghetto resident or policeman in depth or been inside a prison. Many criminology professors and researchers come directly to their university posts possessed of little or no experiential background in the subject areas in which they will be involved as educators. While this does not make effective teaching and research impossible, it is nonetheless a decided handicap. How credible to contemporary students is the expertise of a criminology professor who has had absolutely no experience with crime, criminals, or the criminal justice system beyond the walls of academe? Even criminologists with substantial backgrounds in the criminal justice field may find themselves attempting to construct theories, design research projects, and answer students' 1972 questions on the basis of outmoded 1962 experience and insights. Ideas, theories, and experience as well, tend to quickly ossify and become irrelevant to new realities with the passage of time. The policemen or probation officers who left his profession twenty, or even ten, years ago would find many changes and few similarities today.

There is little question that the ability of scientists to develop original insights and research in their areas of expertise is augmented by current and intimate familiarity with a given field. "Faculty internships" in the criminal justice professions could represent a valuable means whereby criminologists might develop viable experiential backgrounds in areas of academic interest and expertise. The long summer vacations of most university faculty and the availability of governmental and other funding for professional development projects afford an ideal opportunity for interested scientists to develop or "brush up" background experience in the criminal justice field. Practitioners in such areas as corrections and law enforcement appear eager to assist criminologists who wish to "go back to school" in the interest of keeping their teaching and research skills in line with current relevance.

As a case in point to illustrate the feasibility of "faculty internships," the senior author, having no experiential background in law enforcement, not long ago concluded that he could best develop insights into the nature of police culture and personality by interning as a patrolman within a major metropolitan department. Such an agency was contacted, and arrangements quickly made for the author to attend the police academy during evenings and subsequently participate as a patrolman during summer vacation. Comparable educational opportunities for participant observation (Becker, 1958; Schwartz, 1955) in the criminal justice field by interested criminologists are legion, but largely untapped at present.

A final major potential of criminology internships, and one equally unexplored, is the possibility of utilizing such laboratory experiences as an educational device for communicating to students a systematic understanding or overview of the criminal justice field. Anyone who has taught police officers, prison counselors, or other practitioners can readily attest to the myopia which usually characterizes their understanding of how different components of the criminal justice system relate to one another. Thus, e.g. even the criminology educated police officer removes the handcuffs from an arrestee at jail with little grasp of the dynamics which will impinge upon him from this point on as he passes through the adjudication and habilitation phases of the process. Such tunnel vision, of course, makes for a badly disjointed and poorly integrated criminal justice system.

Postinternship seminars, which provide an opportunity for academically supervised interaction between students who have viewed quite disparate parts of the criminal justice system, might prove to be a valuable educational technique for conceptually linked different structures and processes to one another. To recall an earlier example, postinternship students might explore together the significance of the labeling process or minority group membership at different points in the criminal justice system. There is much to be learned in such a setting from the exchange of anecdotes borne of quite diverse internship experiences.

In conclusion, it is the authors' belief that criminology internships, carefully chosen, structured, supervised, and coordinated into the contemporary criminal justice system during the process of formal criminological education, represent a singularly valuable heuristic device. The internship experience provides a controlled interface between criminology as a science that is both theoretical and applied. Whether following his university experience as a practitioner or scientist, the student will have been exposed to this integration of theory and practice, with subsequent recognition of the other's relevance to his understanding of crime and criminal behavior.

REFERENCES

Becker, Howard S.: Problems of inference and proof in participant observation. *Am Soc Rev, 23*:652-660, 1958.

Irvin, John: The prison experience: the convict world. In Carter, Robert M., Glaser, Daniel, and Wilkins, Leslie T. (Eds.): *Correctional Institutions.* Philadelphia, Lippincott Co., 1972.

Johnson, Elmer H.: *Crime, Correction and Society.* Homewood, Dorsey Press, 1968.

Lemert, Edwin M.: *Social Pathology.* New York, McGraw-Hill, 1951.

Pilivan, Irving and Briar, Scott: Police encounters with juveniles. In Rubington, Earl and Weinberg, Martin S. (Eds.): *Deviance: The Interactionist Perspective.* New York, the Macmillan Co., 1968.

Roebuck, Julian and Zalhart, Paul: The problems of educating the correctional practitioner. *J Crim Law, Criminology, Police Sci, 56*:45-53.

Sellin, Thorsten: Culture conflict and crime. *Soc Sci Res Council Bull, 41:* 3, 1938.

Schwartz, Morris S. and Schwartz, Charlotte Green: Problems in participant observation. *Am J Soc, 60*:343-353, 1955.

Wolfgang, Marvin E.: Criminology and the criminologist. *J Crim Law, Criminology, Police Sci, 54*:159-161, 1963.

CHAPTER 8

THE INTEGRATION OF SOCIAL SCIENCES INTO THE FIELDS OF CRIMINOLOGY, LAW ENFORCEMENT, AND CORRECTIONS

PETER C. KRATCOSKI

Professor Kratcoski teaches in the Department of Sociology, Kent State University, Kent, Ohio.

CONDITIONS OF INNER CITY TURMOIL and campus unrest, public fear of crime, and the attention drawn to primitive prison conditions by the mass media led to a demand for more educational programs at all levels in the fields of criminology, law enforcement, and corrections in American colleges and universities during the decade of the sixties. In 1960, only twenty-six institutions offered full-time law enforcement programs at all levels in higher education (Tenney, 1971). However, by 1970 the Law Enforcement Education Directory listed 292 institutions which offered 340 different programs in law enforcement and criminal justice, including 257 associate, fifty-five baccalaureate, twenty-one master's, and seven doctoral programs. Many other colleges and universities offer a specialization in criminal justice or criminology within other degree programs, i.e. sociology or political science, making the actual number of existing programs considerably higher.

Tenney (1971) listed the following factors as contributing to this significant growth: the assassination of President Kennedy, which resulted in a nationwide examination of the pathological features of our legal system which could combine to permit such an occurrence; the Task Force Report of the Commission on Law Enforcement and the Administration of Justice (1967), which recommended an educational emphasis in police work;

and the passage of the Omnibus Crime Control and Safe Streets Act (1968), creating the Law Enforcement Assistance Administration.

The fact that the Law Enforcement Assistance Administration provided curriculum development grants for programs in these areas and funds for student training grants and tuition loans supplied a powerful economic incentive for educational institutions to act quickly. Consequently, many new programs were hastily formulated, some of which had poorly-defined goals and modes of operation and dubious academic quality.

This paper explores the perceptions of faculty members who teach in criminology, law enforcement, or corrections programs concerning the ideal balance of training and general education in the curriculum, the importance of social science courses in the programs, and the best types of academic or professional preparation for effective teaching in these areas.

RELATED RESEARCH. Recent research studies (Karacki and Galvin, 1968; International Association of Chiefs of Police, 1968; Tenney, 1971; Eastman, 1972) have explored the number and level of programs available, their curriculum design, the number of full- and part-time students and faculty members, faculty members' professional qualifications and experience, textbooks used, and admissions policies.

Tenney, in *Higher Education Programs in Law Enforcement and Criminal Justice* (1971), developed a model to categorize programs in the criminal justice field. The rationale for his classificatory scheme was based on an analysis of the curriculum offerings. Twenty-eight new programs funded by the Office of Law Enforcement Assistance curriculum development grants were surveyed. The three distinct types of programs he delineated were labeled training, professional, and social science. The training oriented program is primarily designed to teach the mastery and application of rules, the development of mechanical skills in the operation of equipment, and the development of skill in the performance of routine maneuvers. The social science oriented program presents the study of social and political institutions from a general theoretical perspective. This program does not specifically prepare a man for work in the subject area.

The professionally oriented program is designed to provide a foundation of expertise in particular subject areas, but to go beyond job training in its concern for the internalization of values, societal goals, and a perspective which does not treat the criminal justice system in isolation. Tenney implied that the professional orientation rests on the middle ground between the differences in philosophy and emphasis which exist between the training and social science programs.

There is strong evidence that the new two-year programs, generally established at junior or community colleges, tend to follow the training orientation, while most of the older programs, particularly those housed in social science departments, tend to follow the social science model, and recently developed baccalaureate degree programs, often housed in independent departments, are attempting to follow the professional model.

Of the twenty-eight programs Tenney surveyed, fourteen were categorized as training, and ten of these were two-year programs. The two-year programs are likely to have a heavy training emphasis; the curriculum is often adapted from existing police academy training programs. At times even using the same instructors, there is a reliance on the use of part-time instructors who are also employed as practitioners, and a sizeable portion of the students involved in the two-year programs are already employed in the criminal justice field.

Both the *International Association of Chiefs of Police Survey of Law Enforcement Education* (1968) and Eastman's *Police Education in American Colleges and Universities: A Search for Excellence* (1972) substantiate these points. The IACP survey revealed that 83 percent of the faculty members at institutions offering an associate degree program taught there on a part-time basis, and 87 percent of these part-time faculty members were currently working with police, courts, or some law enforcement agency (Tenney, 1971). Eastman in 1970 found that two-year programs enrolled about 75 percent of all law enforcement students, 52 percent of the students were enrolled part-time, and 48 percent of the students were currently employed in the field. Since the two-year programs are often located in junior or community colleges, the administrators of the specific agencies for which the students work may also serve as part-time faculty members. In these cases they can exert a strong influence on curriculum design.

The Eastman study surveyed police administrators regarding the type of background they preferred for those they hired. They were in general agreement that individuals with law enforcement degrees made the best candidates for employment and that recruitment programs for police departments should be aimed at this group. They evidently did not consider liberal arts or social science graduates to be as desirable as those who had more specific training in law enforcement.

In Tenney's survey of twenty-eight new programs, only two fit his social science category. Both of these were four year programs. Also, of the 340 programs listed in the 1970 *Law Enforcement Education Directory,* only nineteen were offered within social science or sociology departments.

This trend away from housing criminology, law enforcement, and corrections programs within social science or sociology departments is somewhat surprising in view of the well-established place of criminology courses within social science and sociology departments. Thirty years ago criminology ranked fifth in the list of most offered courses in sociology departments (Kennedy and Kennedy, 1942). A comparable 1971 survey revealed that 68 percent of the 537 institutions contacted incorporated one or more courses in criminology or penology in their undergraduate programs, and criminology-penology ranked sixth in the list of most offered courses (Reid and Bates, 1970).

There are several explanations why the new programs did not develop within the existing social science departments. In the middle sixties, when many dramatic law and order confrontations occurred, there was a search for quick, easily implemented solutions. The available sociological solutions to these problems called for broad, structural changes in the political and economic systems of the community which would require years of effort to put into effect and which would not yield immediate visible results.

In addition, social science department courses in criminology and corrections are rarely designed to be direct training for employment in the fields of law enforcement and criminal justice. Karacki and Galvin's survey of sociology departments which offered criminology and corrections courses revealed that relatively few of the students in these courses were actually studying to be practitioners, and that the students perceived the major purposes of the courses to be providing them with a general background in the social sciences. Only occasionally did the faculty members who taught those courses feel that their main purpose was to directly prepare their students for employment in the field. In fact, several sociologists who taught criminology expressed an aversion for correctional work.

Given the combination of the search for programs in which direct dramatic effects would be evident, and the social science departments' reluctance to specialize in the development of practical, professional-training programs, it is not difficult to understand why the new programs tended to develop in independent departments.

Tenney found that five of the twenty-eight programs he studied fit his professional classification, and that seven others had either a combination of the training and professional or professional and social science orientations.

On the basis of Tenney's categorizations, one would suspect that recently developed four-year programs are likely to be based in independent departments, and to be attempting to balance the job training orientation and the more theoretical focus characteristic of programs in social science departments. Accordingly, it was decided to undertake a survey of four-year baccalaureate programs in criminology, law enforcement, and corrections to look for evidence of such a trend not only in new programs but also in long established ones. It was also decided to solicit this information directly from faculty members in the programs, who may or may not be in agreement with current policies set by the programs' administrators. The faculty members were asked their opinions about the orientations these programs should follow with regard to the balance of training and theoretical courses and the type of background (academic or professional) which was the best preparation for teaching in these areas. Data regarding the educational and professional backgrounds of the faculty members and about the focus and curriculum design of the program at their college were also gathered.

PROCEDURE. A questionnaire was sent to each faculty member of forty-six college and university departments listed in the 1970 *Law Enforcement Education Directory* as offering four year baccalaureate programs in criminology, law enforcement, or corrections. No claim is made that this survey presents a complete picture of the programs in American colleges and universities today, since faculty lists were not available or were incomplete for some of the colleges listed. In addition, Eastman's findings, released after this survey was conducted, reveal that the number of programs is substantially higher than the 1970 *Law Enforcement Education Directory* indicated. Also complicating the selection of survey participants was the fact that faculty members in law enforcement, criminology, or corrections programs which were attached to other departments, i.e. sociology, were not listed separately in the college catalogs from which the faculty lists were compiled. In these cases questionnaires were sent to all department members, and, when ascertainable, the names of those not connected with the law enforcement, corrections, or criminology programs were eliminated from the sample.

On May 15, 1972, 489 questionnaires were mailed to all faculty members who might be involved in these programs at forty-six of the fifty-five colleges listed in the Directory. A follow-up appeal letter was sent to nonrespondents two weeks later. One hundred one faculty members were later eliminated on the basis of information received from respondents that they were not involved in these programs, twenty-eight returned their questionnaires uncompleted because they were no longer teaching in the field or had changed positions, and another twenty-four questionnaires were returned unopened because the addressee could not be located. After these corrections, an amended sample of 336 remained.

SAMPLE. One hundred twenty-nine faculty members from forty-four of the forty-six colleges and universities contacted completed the survey instrument. The titles of the baccalaureate programs at these institutions, as reported by the faculty members, indicated that twenty-three of the programs were in general criminal justice, ten implied a law enforcement or police science specialization, seven implied general criminology, three corrections, and one social science. A number of these institutions also had associate degree programs, graduate programs, or both. Twenty-six of the programs were housed in independent departments, while eighteen were attached to another department, with seven attached to political science, four to social science, three to public administration, and one each to psychology, education, law, and the evening college. The programs required an average of 10.6 courses in the major subject area and 8.8 courses in the social sciences. The full-time to part-time faculty ratio at these institutions, as reported by the faculty members, was almost one to one (298 full-time, 292 part-time).

Ninety-eight percent of the respondents were male. Their mean age was forty-three years, and their mean years teaching in the fields of corrections, law enforcement, or criminology was eight years. Eighty-seven percent were full-time faculty members, and 13 percent were part-time.* Forty-five percent of the respondents held doctorates, 8 percent were Juris Doctors, 1 percent were M.D.'s, 40 percent held master's degrees, and 6 percent had baccalaureate degrees only. Thirty-eight percent stated that they had specifically prepared for teaching positions in these fields at either or both the undergraduate or graduate level, while 62 percent had a more general educational background. Eighty-four percent had experience in the field, with nearly half of the respondents having experience in a number of different types of criminal justice work. Nineteen percent currently were teaching courses in other departments in addition to their work in criminology, law enforcement, or criminal justice programs.

PROGRAM ORIENTATIONS. Eighty-one percent of the respondents stated that the predominant emphasis of their institutions' programs was on general education in the criminal justice field. Twelve percent regarded specific job training as the predominant emphasis, and 7 percent declared that their programs provided for both. One must conclude that most of the respondents per-

---

* It was obvious from the respondents' reports of the number of part-time faculty members at their institutions that many of these were not listed in the college catalogs, and therefore had not been included in the survey.

ceived their programs as encompassing much more than job training. The professional model characterization of programs delineated by Tenney appears to be appropriate for most of the programs covered in the survey.

Faculty members were also asked to describe the dominant concentration of their programs' subject matter content. Seventy-one percent said it was broadly oriented to the entire criminal justice system, including courses in law enforcement, the judicial process, and corrections. Twenty-one percent stated that law enforcement, police science, or police administration dominated, 6 percent named corrections, and 2 percent cited other emphases. The high percentage of programs oriented to the entire criminal justice system indicates that these programs are quite different from the typical two-year programs analyzed by Tenney, Eastman, and the IACP survey, which tended to be chiefly law enforcement oriented.

When asked to specify the types of work or agencies for which these programs prepared students, 75 percent of the respondents mentioned two or more criminal justice fields, again revealing the broad, general orientation of most of the programs. Seventeen percent stated that their programs prepared students specifically for work in police departments, 5 percent listed correctional work, and the remainder named community programs or teaching in the field.

The respondents were asked to give their opinions about the criteria on which a viable program in corrections, law enforcement, or criminology should be built. To accomplish this they were asked to express their agreement or disagreement with statements pertaining to recruitment and qualifications of faculty, the orientation of subject matter (specific training or more general education), and the utility of having a college degree as preparation for a career in corrections, law enforcement, or criminology. Available responses included "strongly disagree," "disagree," "uncertain," "agree," and "strongly agree."

Table 8-I shows faculty responses to key items, with the "strongly disagree" and "disagree," and "agree" and "strongly agree" responses combined in the table.

As shown in Table 8-I, the highest faculty consensus was on

TABLE 8-I

FACULTY RESPONSES TO PROGRAM AND FACULTY
ORIENTATION ITEMS
(Percentages)

Item	Agree	Uncertain	Disagree
A strong background in the social sciences is an absolute necessity for practitioners in these fields	86	5	9
A good program in criminology, law enforcement, or corrections should include courses designed to give field experience and placement within an agency to students	81	10	9
The major orientation of programs in these fields should be on offering general knowledge about the subject matter rather than preparing the student for a specific job within the fields	80	5	15
The practical training for work in law enforcement and corrections should be handled by the police academies or through on the job training rather than included in college and universities' programs .	64	10	26
Criminology, law enforcement, and corrections programs should strongly emphasize the practical and operational aspects of the field	34	10	56

the absolute necessity for practitioners to have a strong background in the social sciences, with 86 percent of the respondents expressing agreement. When the faculty members in independent departments were compared with those in programs attached to another department, those attached to another department were slightly higher in their percentage of agreement (89% to 84%). There was also strong agreement by the general sample that programs should provide students with experience in the field while pursuing the program (81%), that the major orientation of these programs should be offering a general knowledge about the subject matter rather than specific job training (80%), and that practical training for work in these fields should be handled by police academies or on the job training rather than within college or university programs (64%). The majority of the faculty members (56%) disagree with the idea that criminology, law enforcement, and corrections programs should strongly emphasize the practical and operational aspects of the field.

The major differences in faculty perceptions on the desired orientation of the programs emerged when full- and part-time faculty members were compared. The part-time faculty members were much more likely to express the opinion that these programs should have a strong emphasis on practical aspects of criminal justice work (53% of the part-time faculty members agreed, compared to 31% of the full-time). The part-time faculty members were substantially less likely to view a social science background as an absolute necessity for practitioners (59% of the part-time faculty members agreed, compared to 90% of the full-time). Only 47% of the part-time faculty members agreed that practical training should be handled by police academies or on the job training rather than included in a college or university program, compared to 78 percent of the full-time faculty respondents.

Although the respondents wanted their students to receive a general orientation to the criminal justice field, they also expressed the opinion that it is important that the students be exposed, through field placement courses, to the actual operation of the system in which they will be employed. In the same vein, the majority of the respondents indicated that they were not interested in presenting a program which followed a predominantly theoretical orientation. Fifty-nine percent did not feel that the thrust of criminology, law enforcement, and corrections programs should be predominantly theoretical.

Faculty views were also obtained regarding the best qualifications for quality teaching performance in these higher education programs. There is considerable sentiment among practitioners that concrete experience in the field is a vital prerequisite for teachers in such programs (see Eastman, 1972). Although 84 percent of the faculty members in our sample had experience in the field, 53 percent felt that higher education is preferable to practical experience as preparation for these faculty positions. Among the part-time faculty members, 29 percent agreed that higher education is preferable, compared to 57 percent of the full-time faculty members. Fifty-nine percent of the general faculty sample agreed that faculty members should be hired for their instructional proficiency rather than for their practical experience.

The respondents in general felt that faculty members, regardless of their experience in these fields, should have academic qualifications. Only 33 percent felt that the academic requirements for faculty members should be relaxed in order to open up opportunities for experienced practitioners to fill faculty positions. The faculty members were apparently concerned about the academic respectability of their programs and with their department's college or university-wide reputation. An indication of these concerns is the fact that 80 percent of the respondents were members of professional associations, 67 percent had published one or more journal articles, 57 percent had authored one or more books, and 74 percent had given one or more papers at professional meetings.

SUMMARY. The findings of this survey suggest that the social science program, with its emphasis on understanding the effects social, environmental, and cultural variables have on deviant behavior, and the training-oriented program, with its emphasis on enforcement techniques and detection and apprehension of criminals, are both falling short of the ideal balance between theory and practice needed for a viable program in the criminology, law enforcement, and corrections fields.

However, changes in criminal justice education are apparent, the public's near paranoia about security, safety, and law and order, which characterized the middle and late sixties has been tempered, and the hastily established two-year programs designed to quickly upgrade policemen's skills are now being reexamined. There is some evidence that the four-year and graduate programs will begin to receive a sizeable portion of new students in criminology, law enforcement, and corrections, while the enrollment in two-year programs will level off. Eastman (1972) found that while the increase in enrollment for students in two-year programs in criminology, law enforcement, and corrections was 30.14 percent from 1967 to 1970, the increase in enrollment for the same period for students involved in four-year programs was 43.09 percent, 32.32 percent for master's students, and 69.2 percent for doctoral students.

Not only is the climate right for a broadly based, professionally oriented type of program, as shown by this survey, but it is clear that those programs which have gained some reputation for excellence, including those at Florida State University, Southern Illinois University, and the University of Southern California, have tended to follow a multidisciplinary or inter-disciplinary approach. Such programs give students the general qualifications to perform in a variety of positions in these fields, and at the same time offer a thorough grounding in the socio-logical theories of crime and delinquency causation and methods of control.

It is noteworthy that several American law schools, including those of the University of Denver, the University of Buffalo, Northwestern University, and the University of Wisconsin, have recognized the fact that a student's knowledge of the law and its application is incomplete unless he has obtained some basic understanding of its place in the larger perspective of society, urbanization, urban change, politics, and behavioral science, and have developed programs which focus on the integration of the fields of law and the social sciences. In the same way, higher edu-cation programs in criminology, law enforcement, and correc-tions can contribute significantly to understanding and con-trolling the problems of contemporary American society if their students are exposed to these problems and trained to treat them within the academically sound context of an interdisciplinary, professionally oriented program grounded in the social sciences.

REFERENCES

Eastman, Esther M.: *Police Education in American Colleges and Universi-ties: A Search for Excellence.* Washington, U.S. Department of Health, Education, and Welfare, 1972.

Karacki, Boren and John J. Galvin: *A Survey of Degree Programs in Crim-inology and Corrections.* Washington, Joint Commission on Correctional Manpower and Training, 1968.

Kennedy, R. and Kennedy, R. J.: Sociology in American colleges. *Am Sociol Rev,* 7:661-675, 1942.

Law Enforcement Education Directory. Washington, International Associa-tion of Chiefs of Police, 1970.

Reid, Sue Titus and Bates, Alan P.: Undergraduate sociology programs in accredited colleges and universities. *Am Sociolog,* 2:165-175, 1970.

Tenney, Charles W., Jr.: *Higher Education Programs in Law Enforcement and Criminal Justice.* Washington, U.S. Government Printing Office, 1971.

CHAPTER 9

CRIMINOLOGY AND A CENTER FOR CRIMINAL JUSTICE: ONE MODEL

RICHARD D. KNUDTEN

Professor Knudten is Director, Center for Criminal Justice and Social Policy, Marquette University, Milwaukee, Wisconsin.

INTRODUCTION

IN RECENT YEARS, since the advent of federal funding of the Omnibus Crime Control and Safe Streets Act of 1968, the question of the nature and direction of teaching and research in the field of criminology and criminal justice has taken on new urgency. Although programs in criminology and/or police science existed previously within schools of social welfare, departments of sociology, law enforcement training agencies, correctional psychology departments, correctional agencies and other bodies, a major expansion of effort in these areas has been stimulated by the creation of the Law Enforcement Assistance Administration's (LEAA) programs in manpower development, including the Law Enforcement Educational Program (LEEP) and the Centers of Excellence in Criminal Justice Program. At present more than 900 colleges and universities, local, regional, and even national in scope and commitment, disperse LEEP funds to students for tuition and other requisites of their academic experience. While the Centers for Criminal Justice have not yet been funded, nearly fifty institutions are vying for Center of Excellence support. Who will be funded and when funding will commence is as yet indefinite. However, the program possesses such value that it is likely to be funded in the near future.

ACADEMIC APPROACHES TO THE PROBLEMS OF CRIMINAL JUSTICE: MULTIPLE MODELS

Because of its many faceted dimensions, those interested in providing academic solutions to the problems of criminal justice have proposed doing so within a series of organizational models which take many forms. Among these are:

A. *Centers for Criminal Justice, for Administration of Justice or Other Similar Titles.* A wide variety of institutions including the University of Southern California, Southern Illinois University, Michigan State University, University of Tennessee, Sam Houston State University, University of Alabama, and Marquette University utilize this type of approach. While some of these institutions employ faculty directly within the Center, others share their faculty jointly with established departments, generally in the behavioral sciences. Through the activities of the interdisciplinary Center, the full range of university resources are brought to bear upon problems in criminal justice.

B. *College of Criminal Justice or a Department of Criminology.* This form of organization provides a more focused answer to the need for criminal justice education and research. Among programs currently operative are colleges or departments at the John Jay School of Criminal Justice, State University of New York (Albany), the University of California (Berkeley), Northeastern University, and Florida State University. Its advantage rests in the concentration of skills it brings to bear on the problems of criminal justice, but its disadvantage rests in its tendency to become somewhat isolated from the other disciplines within its and surrounding institutions.

C. *Inter-Departmental Administration of Justice Program.* As an approach, this is less definitive than the preceding two. Instead, it seeks to provide the flexibility of interdisciplinary crossing of disciplines while continuing to be less specialized than either the Centers or the Colleges for Criminal Justice. Bradley University is an example.

D. *The Business Administration Model.* Because of the increasing interest in court administration and questions of public policy, several criminal justice programs have been organized within schools or departments of business admin-

istration (e.g., Duquesne University). While they un-
doubtedly hold some merit, they nevertheless tend to be
somewhat removed from the major thrusts of criminal
justice concern.

E. *The Law School Center.* In recent years several leading
   law schools have taken initiative to create centers for studies of the criminal justice system or in other specialized
   aspects of criminal justice problem areas. Representative
   programs are in operation currently at Boston University,
   University of Mississippi, New York University, University
   of Chicago, University of Tennessee and Marquette University Law Schools. Their emphasis tends commonly to be
   toward concerns common to preservice or in-service legal
   education and research. As such, the behavioral dimensions
   of criminal justice problems frequently become sub-
   merged to legal interests and an integrated approach to the
   problems of criminal justice is not achieved.

F. *The Sociology and/or Educational Sociology Department
   Model.* Historically, the concern for criminal justice matters has been expressed by sociology departments. Heavily
   oriented to behavioral and social science methodology, in-
   structions providing this response pattern have traditionally emphasized the scientific training of teachers and researchers in criminology. The University of Pennsylvania
   provides a good example of this approach, while Wayne
   State University provides insight into an educational sociology model. While the behavioral and social science emphasis inherent in this model provides a necessary ingredi-
   ent to criminal justice methodology and research, the interdisciplinary character of criminal justice problems is
   frequently overlooked.

G. *The Law Enforcement Programs Model.* Generalized law
   enforcement programs have mushroomed in number with
   the funding of the LEEP program. Many are restricted
   to the training of police officers while others include
   the generalized training of court and corrections person-
   el. In many instances, they are serious attempts to assist in

the up-grading of criminal justice personnel while in others the thrust is oriented more toward the acquiring of new sources of institutional revenue. Although some schools have specialized in law enforcement training (e.g., Portland State University, St. Joseph's College (East Chicago), others focus more fully on correctional questions.

H. *A Consortium of Centers Model.* The consortium approach, while rather limited in number, assumes several differing models. For example, the University of Colorado (Boulder) works with the University of Colorado Medical Center (Denver) to establish a wide ranging program. The Atlanta Consortium of the Atlanta University Center, Emory University, Georgia State University, Georgia Institute of Technology, and the University of Georgia stresses a regional approach to the criminal justice issues. The Northeastern Illinois Consortium on Criminal Justice and Social Justice Education, a consortium of many junior, community and four-year colleges provides a more generalized consortium approach. More interesting consortium models are provided by Michigan State University which is working with Wayne State University Law School and Loyola University Department of Social Work to provide an integrated criminal justice and urban experience, and by the Southern Illinois Consortium which includes the University of Illinois (Chicago Circle) and Sangamon State University.

I. *A College of Human Development Model.* This model, conceived by Pennsylvania State University, assumes that the issues of criminal justice are truly ones of human development and can be attacked most properly from this point of view. A weakness of this approach rests with its possible tendency to minimize the legal and criminalistics base of the problem.

J. *A Continuing Education Program Model.* Many institutions offer solutions to criminal justice problems by providing on-going educational (but few research) opportunities to those already practicing in the field through their department or division of continuing education. As an approach, it serves a need; however, if one seeks to bring the total thrust of science to bear upon criminal justice concerns, it remains generally inadequate. Examples of a continuing education model are provided by American University and the various extensions of other state universities.

K. *A Forensic Science Program Model.* A highly specialized model, its central focus is upon the laboratory and forensic science aspects of criminal justice problems. Consequently, it provides a narrow base upon which to build a criminal justice program. Examples of the forensic science thrust are found at Youngstown State University (Ohio) and Georgetown University.

L. *A Social Welfare Model.* Many programs are located within or are associated with schools of social welfare. Consequently, their thrust is frequently oriented to corrections and treatment questions. Often more practitioner and client oriented than science-oriented, the demands for service may over-ride broader criminal justice concerns. The University of Chicago, Florida State University, University of California (Berkeley), and East Carolina University offer illustrations of the social welfare model.

M. *School of Public and Environmental Affairs, Institute of Policy Science and Public Affairs or Other Similar Models.* Focusing less upon the specific problems of criminal justice and more upon elements of social policy and public organization are programs devised at Indiana University, Duke University, University of North Carolina, and University of Southern California.

N. *An Urban Studies Model.* Even more remote from the central concerns of criminal justice are those institutions which approach problems in the administration of justice from the context of their urban studies programs. The sweep of criminal justice concerns becomes one among many elements under study in the urban complex. While an urban approach, however, may offer a unified frame of reference for dealing with the problems of criminal justice, it is more restrictive in scope than is usually a college of criminal justice or a center for administration of justice model. Universities working in this direction include the University of Notre Dame and the University of Texas (Arlington).

O. *The Graduate School Model.* Some institutions, recognizing that the issues and problems of criminal justice cut across both undergraduate and graduate education and research, have created their criminal justice response within the graduate school of the institution. By doing so, they assume that they will be able to mobilize any element of the university, as necessary, to assist in the training and research functions required for the solution of criminal justice problems. Although such an approach may lead eventually to the formation of a center or college of criminal justice, its early orientation is toward an intra-university program utilizing the full research and training capabilities of the various branches of the university itself. The University of Oregon is a representative example of this approach.

P. *Other Specialized Approaches.* In some instances, solutions to criminal justice problems are sought not in the previous ways mentioned but through more regional or specialized approaches. A catch-all category, the specialized approach in effect is an open-ended category. It may involve such specialized agencies as the Western Interstate Commission on Higher Education (WICHE) or other similar regional or governmental groups.

THE MARQUETTE UNIVERSITY MODEL: A CENTER FOR CRIMINAL JUSTICE AND SOCIAL POLICY

In order to capitalize upon the various disciplines and sciences comprising Marquette University, the Marquette Center for Criminal Justice and Social Policy has integrated the elements of Liberal Arts departments (sociology, psychology, history, anthropology, political science, economics) capable of supporting a major program in criminal justice, the Law School and its collateral programs in criminal justice agency organization, minority employment, education and research, medical and health resources through the School of Dentistry, and a working relationship with the Medical College of Wisconsin (formerly Marquette University Medical School), and the schools and/or colleges of Nursing, Education, Engineering, Journalism, Speech, Business Administration, and the Division of Continuing Education in a university-wide approach to criminal justice problems. Between forty-five and fifty-two faculty members have varying degrees of relationship to the operation of the Center.

As conceived within the University, the Center for Criminal Justice is activated by the Director who coordinates various committees and works closely with the Marquette University Advisory Board and appropriate members of the Board of Visitors. Responsible to the Dean of the Graduate School, the Director works in turn with an Administrative Assistant, several Assistant Directors and the professional staff within the program. The facilities and manpower of the Department of Continuing Education are utilized for outreach programs and professional staff for training and research within the criminal justice area. The Administrative Assistant administers daily the operations of the Center in a manner consistent with the University policy and works with the Director to expedite the general Center program.

Professional staff within the program share membership in three basic Center committees of Educational Programs and Materials, Community and Personnel Services, and Research Development Services. Among the tasks given the committee on Educational Programs and Materials are the following:

A. Responsibility for the A.A., A.B., M.A., and Ph.D. programs relating to criminal justice.

B. Forensic programs.

C. Educational materials development through such activities as: (1) correspondence courses, (2) Center publications, (3) speakers series, (4) audiovisual programs, (5) paraprofessionals training program, (6) integration of university departments and schools curricular offerings, and (7) visiting professors program.

Among the Community and Personnel Services opportunities of the Center are:

A. Advisement of indigenous community action programs;
B. Specialized programs of education and training in youth and the law, minorities and the police, trial-sentencing procedures, prosecutor institutes;
C. Volunteer and in-service programs with the University undergraduate and graduate students;
D. Criminal justice personnel placement assistance; and
E. In-service training institutes, seminars and the like.

Included in the responsibilities of the Committee on Research and Development Services are:

A. provision for pure and evaluation research activities;
B. technical, systems analysis and planning studies;
C. consultation services; and
D. research grant development.

Secretarial and research assistant personnel support the Center organization.

While the Marquette model is currently founded upon the released time of faculty members from their particular departments and is not as fully developed as the Center program at Southern Illinois University where appointments are made primarily to the Center itself, the existing approach most fully responds to the current operational policies of Marquette University and provides the foundation upon which future programs may be developed.

PUBLIC POLICY AND CENTERS FOR CRIMINAL JUSTICE

Although Centers for Criminal Justice, whether in the form of the Marquette or some other model, have a major opportunity to serve outside the limits of the educational institutions they are related to by providing the intellectual and research base upon which strategic plans for delinquency and crime prevention and control may be founded, they have tended to date to work independently of each other and often in competition. Where contributions have been made to public policy questions, they have been oriented to crime-specific planning rather than to questions of regional or even national strategy. Too often, the differences in methods and conceptions of the problem have kept line personnel separated from their academic counterparts who can provide needed in-puts into the strategy development process. However, the problems of criminal justice are now so extensive and so serious that the luxury of indifference and the waste of competition can no longer be afforded. While some quarters have been historically suspicious of governmental agency and educational institution linkages, it has become increasingly obvious that meaningful and strategic programs of crime reduction, delinquency control, diversion and deinstitutionalization depend upon the emergence of a closer and more meaningful working relationship of educational and governmental agencies.

In some instances, this relationship has already been effected. The Youth Development and Delinquency Prevention Administration (YDDPA) of the Department of Health, Education and Welfare, for example, has been working closely with Colorado and Fordham Universities to develop a strategy for delinquency prevention. In other instances, other public agencies are only now developing similar relationships with institutions of higher education. The Law Enforcement Assistance Administration of the Department of Justice, for example, has only recently embarked upon its program of definition of Phase III. While in Phase I of LEAA's program agency efforts were directed toward immediate improvements in the criminal justice system through correction of obvious deficiencies, attention during Phase II, continuing even now, has been given to criminal justice planning in its various dimensions. However, Phase III, oriented to primary prevention, diversion, and deinstitutionalization and currently under definition, promises to challenge the educational community to share in the creation and possible implementation of public policy.

If the academic community is to share effectively in this enterprise, the Centers must develop better working relationships with each other and with public agencies. As many segments of the criminal justice system as possible must be mobilized for service. The simple expediency of seeking grants for particularistic research or educational efforts must be widened to include a concern for the stability of society and plans for the reduction of delinquency-crime. Steps in this direction may be taken by revising the formula and reasons for funding LEAA programs throughout the United States and the development of regional and national centers for criminal justice. Although each national and/or regional center would operate its own program, the base this program provides would serve as the foundation upon which important questions of national policy would be examined. While LEEP programs would continue locally to bring educational opportunities to in-service and pre-service students, the creation of a system of regional and national centers would provide the necessary stimulus to upgrade and integrate the level of criminal justice education and research. As regional centers worked actively with national centers for criminal justice to devise regional and national strategies for an integrated approach to criminal justice problems, not only both parties but also the public would benefit. Working in cooperation with representative governmental agencies and the Interdepartmental Council to Coordinate all Federal Juvenile Delinquency Programs, centers sharing in the enterprise may be able to complement the many crime-specific proposals already generated by local and state planning agencies. By sharing cooperatively in this manner, national and regional criminal justice concerns, often overlooked in the rush to complete a particular facet of a research project or governmental program, would be placed in their proper perspective and the basic goals of criminal justice to reduce the number of clients coming to its attention and to divert many currently within its grasp to the community would be enhanced.

CHAPTER 10

COPS IN COLLEGE: OBSERVATIONS ON TEACHING CRIMINOLOGY TO POLICE

———————— JANET HENKIN ————————

Professor Henkin is a member of the Department of Behavioral Sciences, John Jay College of Criminal Justice of the City University of New York, New York.

THE RECENT SUPPORT of higher education for policemen reflects the generally high esteem in which education is held in American society. Although the traditional function of liberal arts education has been expanded, the basic assumption that education improves one's job performance and overall efficiency still remains the general consensus. There have been some dissenting voices largely claiming that a college education for law enforcement personnel is irrelevant, unnecessary, and essentially impossible to achieve (Chevingny, 1969). However, the overwhelming opinion of criminologists, educators, and the general public has strongly supported educational advancement for police officers. Recently, the Police Commissioner of New York City publicly supported the principle of a college education as an eventual requirement for all police under his jurisdiction.

Nevertheless, there has been a glaring absence of empirical data designed to evaluate the effects of college educational opportunities upon the police. Opinions have ranged from a focus upon the negative effects of academic advancement to those which see higher education for police as essential to the alleviation of some of the problems of the increased complexity of police work (Constantine, 1972). The basic philosophy of police progress within the academic community is a strongly held belief that the result of academic training in areas other than traditional police science, police administration, and traffic control will ultimately produce more efficient policemen. The hope has been that the attitudes and knowledge to which police are exposed will greatly supplement their pre-police training that in most instances is "archaic and inane" (Germann, 1971).

Nationally, there are approximately 50,000 police who attend college (Caldwell, 1970). Many of these police-students have benefited from a system of loans and grants provided by the Law Enforcement Educational Program (LEEP). In New York City, Brooklyn College established a police science program in its Division of Vocational Studies, a program duplicated within the year at yet another four year college within the city system. Since the inception in California in 1946 of post-high school training for police, we have seen the proliferation of police science programs throughout the country. Today there are more than 300 such programs for police ranging from an established police science curriculum to those of a traditional liberal arts orientation (Locke and Smith, 1970).

John Jay College of Criminal Justice, where I am presently teaching, is a unique experiment in making available to police officers a four-year bachelors degree and/or two-year associate degrees. At its inception in 1965, more than 90 percent of the John Jay student body were police and correctional personnel. With the introduction of "open enrollment" and the general increase in the demand for higher education within CUNY, that figure has been reduced to approximately 50 percent of the student body. In New York City, approximately 8 percent of the more than 30,000 man police force attend college, most of these at John Jay, where hours and scheduling have deliberately accommodated the policeman's shifting work hours.

When one considers the question of what motivates a policeman to attend college while working full time for the police department, the picture is anything but clear. In New York City and most other large jurisdictions, departmental promotions and appointments are based exclusively upon competitive civil service examinations and departmental excellence. Thus, rewards and recognition by one's peers and superiors within the police force are practically nonexistent when based upon academic achievement. To the contrary, it has been suggested that the reverse may be true. Resentment and distrust of those police who do attend college is a rather common response within the precinct. In addition, according to Niederhoffer's classic study of the New York City police, "there are signs of a growing and abrasive rift between the advocates of higher educational standards and those who oppose any form of professional treatment that is based on academic accomplishment" (Niederhoffer, 1967).

Those who teach police and who have analyzed the unique situation in which a patrolman or officer of higher rank finds himself when in the role of student have agreed rather remarkably on the nature of the "police personality." For the most part, they have not examined the reactions of police when they are exposed to a liberal arts education. The parallel between police traits and authoritarianism has been well researched and is well known. If, as research indicates, police tend to be more suspicious, conventional, cynical, prejudiced, and exhibit greater distrust of what they consider "ivory tower intellectualism," are we wasting our time exposing these officers to the perspectives and methodology of the academic community (Balch, 1971)? Perhaps of greater importance is the question of selectivity process that motivates some police to attend college while the great majority do not. Smith et al. found that police who attend college are significantly less authoritarian than those who do not (Smith, Locke and Walker, 1967). They suggest that this college group will more likely be able to function with greater efficiency when confronted with the growing demands of modern police work. However, a later Smith study, insofar as it deals with *police in college,* contradicts the stereotype of authoritarianism among police. Their tests for traits of authoritarianism among police and non-police college freshmen reveal less authoritarianism among the police freshmen than non-police freshmen (Smith, Locke, and Walker, 1968).

From studies such as the one cited, it would appear that those police motivated to attend a liberal arts college do not necessarily exhibit personality traits generally associated with policemen to the same degree as non-college police. The response of these policemen-students though, when confronted by an academic milieu and with the examination of subjects that deal directly and indirectly with critical analyses of their own occupational identity may create problems not yet adequately defined. I refer specifically to police enrollment and participation in courses of instruction in criminology and juvenile delinquency taught by a behavioral scientist rather than as a component of a police science program.

During the two years that I have been on the faculty of John Jay College of Criminal Justice, I have taught approximately 500 students, and more than half of them were members of the New York City police department or affiliated with a suburban police department. Although the percentage of police students in the total John Jay population is declining, criminology courses and those concerned with social problems, deviance, etc. continue to attract a disproportionate number of police students. In my role as instructor, some interesting behavior and attitudinal patterns have become apparent. These reactions appear to be independent of the students' innate intelligence and intellectual capacity. I cannot however claim to have neutralized the Heisenberg effect, since reaction to my own teaching methods and personality has not been calculated.

My police students have generally reflected the ethnic and racial composition of the New York City Police Department with the decided exception of the percentage of black policemen. The predominantly Irish and German ethnicity supplemented with a sizable number of Italian-Americans comprised the bulk of the police portion of the classes. However, there seemed to be a disporportionate number of black police officers in these classes, although the Smith study of the John Jay student population does not indicate any such imbalance (Smith, Locke, and Walker, 1967).

As one who has taught criminology to police and non-police students at that branch of CUNY specifically designed to accommodate the college-oriented policeman, I have had the opportunity to both teach and communicate with a unique student population. I must at this time state that like most of the general public, I had accepted the stereotype of the typical policeman so popular today in the academic world. How then to impart knowledge and a desire to learn among police students. I was initially concerned with teaching a behavioral scientist's approach to students who were *a priori* rigid and anti-intellectual. Even harder then, to teach police a subject that each of them felt he already knew through his experience and in which each was a self-styled expert. It became clear that acceptance of the content of the course was dependent upon several factors. These included:

a) the ability of the instructor to establish and maintain rapport with a group of students who have brought with them to the class in criminology the hostility and suspicion reserved for the academic community in general and for non-police personnel and social scientists in particular.

b) the ability of the police students to attain temporary role-distance from being cops while in class.

c) the minimizing of role-conflict particularly when discussing police activities, defining situations and discussing causal factors in crime and delinquency, especially when these explanations seemed to conflict with their stereotypes and on-the-job experience.

I have found it extremely useful to use the police officers' consciousness of kind to neutralize the defensiveness and self-consciousness that sometimes occurs in the classroom. This is especially urgent in classes containing police and non-police students. The intense dislike and suspicion that some non-police students display for police, and the sight of an off-duty patrolman, recognizable to all with his service revolver in plain sight, does little to create unity within the classroom. The mandatory carrying of weapons automatically distinguishes police from non-police, a label that has at times proven disfunctional. It has been my experience that once the initial shock of being taught criminology by a non-police officer and by a *woman* wears off, their receptivity slowly increases. Obviously, individual personality and temperamental differences will become apparent. Although Smith et al. found no greater degree of authoritarianism when comparing police and non-police freshmen, my own experience based upon teacher-student interaction and observation of police and non-police student exchanges raises serious questions about their conclusions (Smith, et al., 1968). It must be noted, however, that the Smith study dealt entirely with college freshmen. Criminology students at John Jay have attained the minimal class standing of sophomores, although class standing has not previously been used as a variable in measuring authoritarianism and other traits.

My strongest impression in the teaching of criminology to both police and non-police students is the seemingly greater lack of ability among police students to disassociate themselves from their occupation while in a classroom situation. This lack of role-distance has proven disfunctional to the learning process; it reinforces defensiveness that seriously hampers the student's ability to critically examine the material and to benefit from class lectures and discussion. This hostility may take various forms, running the gamut from the argumentative and overtly hostile policeman who is unable to consider any analyses that differ from his own personal experiences to the police-student who will sit sullenly in class for the entire semester in a posture conveying his disgust and lack of confidence in the subject matter. In my experience, age has not been a critical factor nor has departmental rank in determining the degree of receptivity to the social sciences as a legitimate approach to the problems of crime, law enforcement, and criminal justice. The critical variable of age has been seen as a factor in police authoritarianism by the Smith research, however (Smith, et al., 1968).

We know that college experience generally affects and may alter some of the values with which students enter the academic community. Certainly part of this transition is a function of the maturation process. When dealing with police students who generally enter and complete their undergraduate education at a later age, the question of the degree and direction of change and flexibility has not yet been determined. In addition, the degree to which these values may be negated by the organizational character of an employer has not yet been established (Klingelhofer, 1965). The question becomes of even greater interest when it concerns policemen and attitudinal change within a relatively liberal intellectual milieu. It has been suggested that when liberals become policemen, they are not likely to remain on the force, reinforcing an already operative self-selective process that weeds out liberals from general recruitment for police forces (Balch, 1971).

Due to the fact that police departments are overwhelmingly white, most of the studies concerned with police personality, measurements of authoritarianism, and nonliberal orientation of police do not consider race as a critical variable. My experience, although limited, raises serious questions concerning the application of what we consider police personality traits to the black policeman insofar as these traits are manifest in a classroom situation. I suggest that the black policeman does not, in his role as student, relate to the world around him, a world that includes police and non-police students, the instructor, and the material under analysis in quite the same way as white policemen do. These differences have been extremely obvious, and I believe are mainly due to a distinctly black orientation to police work and to American society itself. A recent study indicates that black policemen are motivated to enter police work "more by the lack of alternative opportunities and by the relative absence of discrimination in civil service employment than by any positive characteristics to be found in police work itself" (Alex, 1969). In addition, it is entirely possible that the individual experiences one has with police while growing up may serve to rid the black policeman of many of the illusions of justice and equal protection under the law.

It would appear that black policemen are more receptive to criticisms of the accepted institutions of American society. This includes the police themselves as well as the entire system of criminal justice which is the basis of considerable analysis in a criminology course. Black policemen in general appear to be less defensive when faced with criticism of police administration and inequities in police behavior and reporting. They do not appear reluctant to discuss in general terms the matter of police corruption, an issue of extreme sensitivity in recent months. Within the classroom situation, the strong antagonism between black and white police has erupted more than once. I have personally "moderated" extremely heated discussions between black and white officers precipitated by what the black policeman felt was the whites' inability to objectively evaluate and respond to a situation where blacks are involved. Indeed, the whole subject of objectivity in police work is usually strongly defended by the white officer, despite strong empirical and theoretical evidence to the contrary.

Overall, the black policeman appears to exhibit less role conflict when assuming the role of student. This may in part account for his greater receptivity of causal analyses of crime and deviance and a generally less rigid approach to the entire field of criminal and delinquent behavior. As a group, the black policemen having entered police work with fewer illusions and for somewhat different reasons seem less threatened by an understanding of the workings of American society within which criminality and deviance exist. His greater dissatisfaction with the status quo seems to increase his ability to divorce himself, if only temporarily, from the role of law enforcement officer.

Although the preceding observations are based upon my own experiences teaching policemen at John Jay College of Criminal Justice, they appear to raise several questions concerning the viability of teaching criminology to policemen under the conditions that presently prevail. The vast body of knowledge has been concerned with authoritarianism and police personality. I suggest that this research be supplemented by an additional focus upon the problems created for the policeman who must temporarily assume the more passive role of student within the academic community. At its mildest, role-conflict may cause resentment and defensiveness. At its worst, role-conflict can neutralize and even negate any positive results of exposure to the behavioral scientist's approach to criminology. With the increased pressure upon police to deal with problems of social unrest and mass demonstrations in addition to a rising crime rate, the importance of college training becomes clear. To ignore the unique problems created for police by role-conflict and ambivalence will only serve to postpone the goal of increased professionalism among our present and future law enforcement personnel.

REFERENCES

Alex, Nicholas: *Black in Blue: A Study of the Negro Policeman.* New York, Appleton-Century-Crofts, 1969.

Balch, Robert: The police personality: fact or fiction? *J Crim Law, Criminol, Police Sci, 63:*1, 1971.

Caldwell, William E.: LEEP: its development and potential. *Police Chief,* 37:24-30, 1970.

Chevigny, Paul: *Police Power: Police Abuses in New York City.* New York, Pantheon, 1969.

Constantine, Thomas A.: Higher education for police: some operational difficulties. *Police Chief, 39:*18-20, 1972.

Germann, A. C.: Changing the police the impossible dream. *J Crim Law, Criminol, Police Sci, 63:*417, 1971.

Klingelhofer, Edwin L.: Studies of the general education program at Sacramento State College. *Technol Bull, 14:* - , 1965.

Locke, Bernard and Smith, Alexander B.: Police who go to college. In Niederhoffer, Arthur, and Blumberg, Abraham S. (Eds.): *The Ambivalent Force: Perspectives on the Police,* Waltham, Ginn and Co., 1970.

Niederhoffer, Arthur J.: *Behind the Shield.* Garden City, Doubleday and Co., 1967.

Smith, Alexander B., Locke, Bernard, and Walker, William: Authoritarianism in college and non-college oriented police. *J Crim Law, Criminol, Police Sci, 58:*128-132, 1967.

————: Authoritarianism in police college students and non-police college students. *J Crim Law, Criminol, Police Sci, 59:*440-443, 1968.

PART THREE

THE EXPANDING ROLE OF CRIMINOLOGICAL EDUCATION

CHAPTER 11

CRIMINOLOGY AS ONE OF THE LIBERAL ARTS

───────────Sawyer F. Sylvester, Jr. ───────────

Professor Sylvester teaches at the Department of Sociology, Bates College, Lewiston, Maine. Professor Sylvester is also Secretary-Treasurer of the American Society of Criminology.

Marc Van Doren has said that the liberal arts are the "maturing rituals of our civilized tribe." The Trivium and the Quadrivium and their modern descendants have always been properly viewed as education rather than training, and as preparing the student to be a cultured member of society rather than merely a jobholder. One might well ask what criminology could contribute to such a grand design.

Criminology can be taught for a number of quite varied reasons: to prepare students, for example, for empirical research in crime, or to train persons for the various specific roles in the criminal justice system. These two functions are perhaps best performed by the graduate school in the first case and the law school or school of criminal justice in the second.

However, one may also teach criminology to sensitize people generally to the inevitable presence of crime in contemporary society and its proper scope and aspect; to prepare the educated citizen for his responsibilities in regard to the criminal offender, unclouded by myth and ignorance and tempered by good sense; or to amplify the scholar's awareness of the place of criminological theory in the history of ideas and the role of crime in the history of events. These latter tasks would seem to be best done in a college of liberal arts.

The teaching of criminology in the United States has from the beginning been much closer to the liberal arts curriculum than in Europe. On the continent, criminology has been generally associated with the more isolated professional disciplines of law or medicine. In the United States, however, criminology has characteristically been a part of the sociology curriculum which, in turn, has been part of the latter-day liberal arts and sciences. It may not be too fanciful to suggest that the ecological emphasis of the first major school of American sociology at the University of Chicago may have been of aid in sociology's being accepted to the degree it has within the liberal arts. It is somewhat more certain that the same ecological stance prompted the early inclusion of crime among the areas of interest of Chicago sociologists.

Sociology has come to be extensively developed in American colleges and universities and at the same time has itself given increasing attention to the problem of crime. Moreover, as the study of society generally has been given financial support in America, so also has criminology; whereas in Europe, the latter having been a peripheral discipline to law or medicine, it has not enjoyed the same degree of assistance. Finally, the more highly empirical approach of American criminology—as contrasted to the more theoretical of the European—can partially be accounted for by its inclusion in sociology, which itself has developed as a notably empirical discipline in America.

The setting of criminology within the liberal arts has had a number of consequences for its teaching and for its teachers. Enrico Ferri referred to criminology as a "synthetic" science, one that is not a primary discipline in itself but borrows, to a greater or lesser extent, from other sciences. It has thus been of considerable advantage to criminology to be taught in a setting where these other sciences were closely available, and where new developments in such other sciences were ready-at-hand. Furthermore, the varied methodology of criminology has included the widest range of historical, observational, and statistical techniques: techniques best learned by an exposure to the similarly varied fields of the liberal arts and sciences.

Criminology as taught to undergraduate students is likely to emphasize fundamental questions of phenomenology, history—intellectual and empirical—philosophy, and jurisprudence; and the "works-of-great-thinkers" approach rather than the narrowly pragmatic. It is precisely this sort of criminological teaching which can be done most profitably in a setting which also acquaints the student with major writers in other peripheral but related disciplines: an acquaintanceship not as easily come by in other than a liberal arts program.

The liberal arts setting also has some consequences for the teacher of criminology. First of all, at least in the smaller liberal arts college, one whose specialty is criminology may, nonetheless, be required to teach in other areas of sociology. This may be experienced by some as a burden; but, on the other hand, it does serve to widen the intellectual horizons of the teacher. Such a teacher may serve as an anchor on overspecialization in criminology itself; and his students, first exposed to the study of crime in such a setting, may thus be deferred from too early concentration. Such a criminologist also teaches initially less specialized students and is encouraged thus to relate criminological questions to the wide variety of their intellectual interests. He also must do more teaching per se, rather than guiding the already-established research interests of his students, as he might in a graduate school. Finally, for good or ill, the liberal arts teacher of criminology is proselyter for the discipline. The egalitarianism of higher education in America guarantees that a substantial proportion of young men and women attain a baccalaureate degree. This coupled with the fact that criminology is generally found in undergraduate sociology curricula ensures that a rather large number of people will be exposed to the principles of criminal science, some of which may find therein an intellectual or professional calling.

Teaching criminology in a liberal arts college is not without its problems, however. The independent college without professional schools, though having close contacts within the liberal arts disciplines, does not have as easy access as the large university to professional fields closely relevant to criminology—notably law, medicine, and psychiatry—nor to their library resources. The same independent college, not having a graduate program, is not able to promote the more sophisticated research of the graduate student which, as an on-going activity, is useful to any criminology program. The understandably greater emphasis on teaching appropriate to the liberal arts college, and the correspondingly larger teaching loads, together with the peripheral committee work which is often a feature of small colleges, tend to limit the amount of faculty research which can be undertaken. In addition, such colleges do not have, nor can they generally attract, funds for criminological research equivalent to the large university. Finally, the small liberal arts college can probably only afford one person with a specialization in criminology, and being the sole criminologist, he may feel a lack of community-of-interest with other scholars in his specialty.

I should now like to consider what I would judge to be some of the advantages of criminology for the liberal arts graduate: first, for the graduate who does not plan to enter the field of criminal justice; and then, for the one who does. Perhaps most obvious (and hence most often overlooked) is the fact that one may study criminology as a student of the liberal arts for the pure intellectual satisfaction of knowing something about crime and the attitudes toward it. After all, is it not a major premise of liberal education that knowledge may be a goal unto itself? Why not then criminological knowledge? Beyond this, if liberal education is principally concerned with the nature of man and his works, as it claims, then the nature and works of criminal man (in the general, not necessarily the Lombrosian, sense) should be included.

Criminology can teach the necessity of scientific detachment and the use of scientific methodology within an area of human behavior often charged with emotion, and can encourage in this area—and, by example, in others—efforts to distinguish the factual from the doctrinaire. The wider dissemination of criminological knowledge at an undergraduate level in the liberal arts may aid in producing a citizenry disabused of the nonsense which still makes up much of the popular understanding of crime and aware that many of the criminal troubles with which our civilization is beset are deeply woven into its history, are vastly complex, and are unlikely to be quickly or completely eliminated.

The state of our prisons, for example—recently (though periodically) disclosed—will never be changed by penologists alone, however expert they may become, without the existence of an educated public which is sensitive to and aware of the problems involved in the treatment of offenders. In addition, an uneducated public seldom promotes research; moreover, it is intolerant of research which fails, as—quite understandably—much of it does.

Having looked at a few of the contributions of criminology to liberal arts education, let us now consider some of the benefits of liberal education to those planning a career in criminology or criminal justice. If the modern theoretical perspective in criminology has taught anything, it is that there is no unitary definition of crime. Law violation exists in all major institutional areas of our society and is manifested by persons of varying constitutional circumstances. Given this, it requires a familiarity with a broad range of disciplines to understand adequately the causes of such diverse phenomena. Most graduate programs in criminology are found in departments of sociology. These, nonetheless, are likely to seek the liberal arts graduate as the most promising candidate for advanced degrees. But even as more graduate programs in criminology alone become available, one of the guards against narrow specialization is to require a broad liberal arts preparation prior to graduate study.

The same etiological diversity in crime would demand that anyone dealing with criminal offenders, at any level, should have as full an understanding as possible of the varieties of human behavior. The tendency toward isolationism in the police, for example (understandable at times), makes it especially important to guard against overspecialization in police education and to provide for the ability to see law enforcement as only one part of the larger fabric of social control. The police represent for many the "cutting edge" of officialdom, and the complexity of their task argues against a narrow technical training. As Quinn

Tamm stated: "It is nonsense to assume that the enforcement of the law is so simple that it can be done best by those unencumbered by a study of the liberal arts."

Since in corrections it is today the presumptive goal of those charged with dealing with deviant members of our society to return them to acceptable social roles, it is necessary that those so charged have as wide and complete a knowledge of that society and its traditions as possible. Furthermore, liberal education is especially important for policymakers in these areas who must be sensitive to a broad range of social, economic, and ethical issues. The argument for technical training in law enforcement and corrections to the exclusion of liberal arts education is essentially short-sighted. If persons in these fields perform their tasks in an atmosphere of misconception and error concerning the broader causative factors concerning crime and the elements of change in human behavior, they are unlikely to perform even their technical tasks well.

Criminology taught in liberal arts colleges affords a unique recruitment opportunity for the fields of criminology and criminal justice, in that it exposes to the discipline for the first time precisely those types of students most needed in the graduate schools, law enforcement, and corrections. But such students are not likely to find narrowly conceived programs in law enforcement or corrections very satisfying, even though they may be prepared technically for a job. Such people will have to be offered educational fare of broader and more compelling intellectual content—including consideration of history, philosophy, sociology, and like subjects—to attract and maintain their interests. This, again, is the task of criminology taught as one of the liberal arts.

There seems to be little agreement on what specific correctional techniques "work" (nor, in fact, that any of them "work" in a direct and complete sense). This fact, coupled with the wide variety of such techniques due to the differences in legal systems, differing willingness to experiment, and variation in institutions and financing suggests that it is better to have people broadly and liberally educated for corrections and law enforcement rather than in any limited number of ephemeral techniques. Such people will tend to be more flexible, more given to experimentation, and less likely to have a vested interest in a specific body of rules and procedures.

Finally, one ought to consider the possibility that however important the relation between education and occupation is, disproportionate emphasis may be placed on the "education-for-job" philosophy generally. It is conceivable that many elements of a liberal arts education may influence occupational effectiveness only remotely—if at all. Furthermore, some jobs in law enforcement and corrections (as with many jobs in other fields) may never turn out to be completely fulfilling vocations, despite high-sounding titles and lofty pronouncements of "professionalism." And yet, such jobs may be vital to social welfare. Especially for persons in such occupations may liberal education accomplish its prime historical task, to make their lives fuller and more interesting, offering depth of interest to avocation as well as vocation. To these, as well as all other members of the criminological fraternity at whatever level, the liberal arts offers, at very least, the richness of Western intellectual heritage.

REFERENCES

Germann: Education and professional law enforcement. *J Crim L C P S*, 58:603, 1967.

Jagiello: College education for the patrolman—necessity or irrelevance. *J Crim L C P S*, 62:114, 1971.

Jameson: Quo Vadimus in criminological training. *J Crim L C P S*, 50:358, 1959.

Johnson: Personnel problems of corrections and the potential contribution of the universities. *Fed Prob*, Dec.: 57, 1967.

Joint Commission on Correctional Manpower and Training: *Criminology and Corrections Programs*. Washington, 1968.

Loughrey and Friese: Curriculum development for a police science program. *J Crim L C P S*, 60:265, 1969.

Morris and Powers: *Report of the New England Correctional Manpower and Training Project*. Mass. Correctional Assoc., 1968.

Morris: What's new in educational for correctional work. *Correctional Res*, 13:   , 1963.

Mueller: *Crime, Law, and the Scholars*. Seattle, University of Washington Press, 1969.

Radzinowicz: *In Search for Criminology.* Cambridge, Harvard Univ Press, 1962.

Reckless: American criminology. *Criminology,* 8:4, 1970.

Szabo: The teaching of criminology in universities: a contribution to the sociology of innovation. *Int Rev Crim Pol,* 22:17, 1964.

Tracy: A survey of criminal justice subject-matter baccalaureate programs. *J Crim L C P S,* 61:576, 1970.

The University Teaching of the Social Sciences: Criminology. UNESCO, 1957.

Van Doren: *Liberal Education.* Henry Holt & Co., 1943.

Waldo: Research and training in corrections: the role of the university. *Fed Prob, June:*57, 1971.

Wolfgang: Criminology and the criminologist. *J Crim L C P S,* 54:155, 1963.

Kerr: *The Uses of the University.* Cambridge, Harvard Univ. Press, 1963.

Schmidt: *The Liberal Arts College.* New Brunswick, Rutgers Univ. Press, 1957.

CHAPTER 12

CRIMINOLOGY, JUSTICE AND SOCIETY: THE ROLE OF SCIENCE IN SOCIAL POLICY—A CANADIAN EXAMPLE

DENIS SZABO

Professor Szabo teaches at the International Center for Comparative Criminology, University of Montreal, Montreal, Canada. Professor Szabo is also Director and member of the Executive Committee of the International Society of Criminology.

THE CHALLENGE OF CRIME, OLD AND NEW

THE INCREASE IN ANTI-SOCIAL ACTIVITIES, either in the classical form (robbery with or without violence, fraud, homicide, etc.) or in its new form (drugs, running away from home, violent contestations of the legitimacy of public order, etc.) strikes contemporary societies without discrimination. The choice victims, however, seem to be, without any possible doubt, the parliamentary democracies.

Academic Criminology and Applied Criminology

For a long time jurists and specialists in the behavioral sciences have looked for the causes of crime and their remedies by studying and working on the individual and social causes of delinquency. What may be called "classical" criminology (from the end of the XIXth century to today's authors whose work reached maturity around the middle of this century) was characterized by its efforts to develop the psychogenetic or sociogenetic theories of delinquent behavior. As a remedy, "clinical" or "correctional" criminology (an etymological difference between the continental European and the Anglo-American usage of the terms) strove to reform the application of punishment, particularly within the penal institution. In fact, prison remained the place above all others to which delinquents of all categories were relegated. We can characterize teaching and criminological research of this initial hundred years (1860-1960) as being oriented towards the study of the etiology of delinquent behavior and the reform of the penal institution as well as aiming towards the training, on a complementary basis, of specialists working mainly in the penal field; complementary training in point of fact, the principal discipline was either law, medicine, or more recently psychology and the social sciences.

During the second half of our century, chiefly in searching for the causes and remedies for the new forms of delinquency, some criminologists have put more and more emphasis on the imperfection and malfunction of the system of the administration of justice. The latter represents all the institutions created by law and tradition to ensure the maintenance of order, the equitable solution of conflicts among people, the protection of rights and the carrying out of responsibilities. It deals essentially with organizations such as the police, courts, penitentiaries, community services for the prevention of delinquency, etc. It is increasingly apparent that the imperfections and the dysfunctional character of the components of the administration of justice constitute a major cause for the menace that crime imposes on the life and the socioeconomic and political institutions of contemporary liberal democracies.

This diagnosis gave birth to a new concept of research and of criminological training: To clinical criminology and to correctional "reform" was added the study of the functions of the instruments of justice, their evaluation (including that of their economic dimensions by using "cost/benefit" analysis), and research on the attitudes and opinions of the ordinary man relevant to present laws. In fact, laws express the customs of a community undergoing swift and considerable changes due to successive technological revolutions: Are we still protecting values dear to the majority of citizens? Do we repress behaviors which, under the influence of new conditions, have become prejudicial to collective interests? Many questions, seemingly of capital importance, present themselves in the search for the legitimacy of the actions of public authorities vigorously disputed by certain minorities whose number is on the increase in our contemporary societies.

Criminology and Social Defense

The sociology of law has been traditionally interested in these problems, and the contemporary movement of social defense has directed these preoccupations of academic research towards more precise objectives of social and constitutional policy. Thus, a certain amalgamation is taking place among these various traditions born at the cross-roads of medico-psycho-social sciences (classical criminology), on the one hand, and of penal law, political and administrative sciences and legal sociology (social defense movement), on the other hand. This amalgamation of interests makes of the criminology of the last third of the XXth century, a political and social science whose objectives of applied research aim not only towards discovering new and efficient methods of treatment for adult and juvenile criminals, but also towards drawing up an instrument for planning and adjusting the whole apparatus of social protection to the changing needs of a society in rapid evolution.

This awareness, which took place simultaneously in various intellectual circles in the world, was emphasized at the "XVIIth International Course in Criminology" which was held in Montreal under the auspices of the International Society of Criminology. The Proceedings entitled "Criminology in Action" bear witness to the coming together of opinions from both sides of the Atlantic. Thus we witness the consolidation of the concerns of traditional scientific criminology with those of social defense movements. Criminology becomes an applied science called upon to contribute to a social policy aimed at a more rational modernization and management of the administration of justice.

This is a three-dimensional discipline: the criminal and his rehabilitation (psychological and clinical criminology); crime conducive societies and policies of social defense (sociological criminology and policies of economic and social improvement); the system of criminal justice and its rational administration (operational research, and administration and planning of justice).

It was originally in this context that the Master's (1960), the Doctoral (1964) and the Bachelor's (1967) programs in criminology were created at the University of Montreal, whose Department (changed to the status of School of Criminology in 1972) teaches these courses.

Criminology at the University of Montreal

Because the teaching of criminology at the University of Montreal started in this intellectual climate, it might be interesting to outline, briefly, the strategy followed in the implementation, academic as well as social, of this new discipline.

We will examine in succession the two fields in which this activity was developed: first in teaching and research, and then in relation to the government and the public.

Teaching

As soon as the new discipline is introduced in the usually conservative milieu of higher teaching, objections are raised on all sides. These objections range from disputing the existence of the discipline itself (define the object, the methods and techniques peculiar to your "science") to questioning the use of the establishment of such a program at the University. Should the orientation be too theoretical, this program would be incorporated within the fundamental human sciences which were always concerned with the study of deviant behavior, whether abnormal or "criminal." Bearing witness to this are the courses in psychology of delinquency, criminal sociology, juvenile delinquency, and the sociology of deviant behavior, etc. offered by the departments of psychology, of sociology, and sometimes of psychiatry or political science. If it is the practical aspect which is emphasized, the link is immediately established, either with the schools of social services or of "psycho-éducateurs" which have special courses for training probation officers and educators of institutionalized juvenile delinquents. The Law Faculty often has resources not to be overlooked for adding courses to its program on penal law.

Nor must we underestimate the objections inspired by a certain option as regards the priorities to be accorded to the solution of social problems. In the opinion of many people, justice comes after education, health, and welfare, to mention but very broad sectors. For which university can presume to have done enough in each of its disciplines to become interested in a new and apparently less important one?

We have to reply in fact to four series of questions: Does criminology as an autonomous discipline exist and can it become the subject of a specific program? Should the answer be in the affirmative; would the criminologist thus trained have his own niche on the labor market? Is criminological research different from other research on crime and delinquency, on legal institutions, etc. undertaken by existing faculties and departments? Would public opinion, the supreme judge in establishing priorities in social policy, accept reforms or changes in the administration of justice?

The answer to these objections voiced by the usual organs of university institutions (board of faculties, special study committees, planning commissions, etc.) was prompted by a series of considerations whose pros and cons are briefly outlined here.

Criminology is an applied discipline drawing on various basic sciences with the object of seeking the causes for criminal behavior in order to arrive at more efficient means of curbing it. Thus, professors of "criminology" will be people trained in medicine, law, or the social sciences who specialized in the study of various types of criminality though always from the viewpoint of how to apply it within the context of the administration of justice. Students of "criminology" will be students who graduated in other disciplines and who wish to specialize for their Master's; they may also be practitioners with a university background wishing to improve their knowledge. These practitioners come from police forces, penal and legal institutions, etc.

In short, criminology is multidisciplinary like medicine, urbanism, or industrial relations; it is applied in the field of treatment of criminals and of crime prevention, which has come to be called "the field of social defense," in the same way as medicine is applied to preserve and improve personal and public health, urbanism to the planning of cities and metropolitan regions, and industrial relations to better labor conditions.

The original students came from various backgrounds, with practitioners making up a good potential for leadership in a sector which in fact is very much lacking in this element. This very theoretically oriented two-year program dealt with groups of thirty to fifty students. Dealing with small classes, the professors were able to elaborate on unpublished teaching texts and to delve into quasi-unknown sectors of applied criminology.

RESEARCH: Soon it was apparent that the arrangement of a doctoral program founded on more thorough research was indispensable if we wanted to prepare our own human resources for higher learning and demonstrate the role of applied human sciences in a more efficient social defense formula. This program was put into effect in 1964 and efforts were made to prepare research projects in order to ensure the funds necessary to full-time studies by candidates in the doctoral program. The Ministries of Social Affairs, Health and Justice, as well as the Canada Council, were funding research in the field of social sciences; some important private organizations like the beer brewers gave funds for research projects. The Ford Foundation presented a grant to make up for the insufficient number of bursaries destined for candidates to the doctoral program. All in all, from 1960 to 1971, more than one million six hundred thousand dollars were spent within the framework of our research projects associated with the expansion of our doctoral program.

These projects have contributed greatly to the creation of the image of the criminologist: a researcher concerned with solving social problems which are becoming increasingly more acute. He can, therefore, be looked upon with consideration by the academic community (research) as well as by those interested in the fact of the social relevance of the university in the modern world (application).

OVERSPECIALIZATION AND SPECIALIZATION: It seems, however, that criminological overspecialization was a partial and insufficient answer to the theoretical analysis of the needs in the field of social defense for specialized professional workers. In fact, as these research studies have shown by helping to clarify the need for action and assistance, we had to turn to the university for specialists to accomplish the tasks thus defined. For example, the professionalization of the police requires recruiting agents at a higher level of proficiency, and the openings for positions of correction, probation and parole officers etc. are multiplying. The question is who is to ensure the training of people at these new intermediate and professional levels. Law faculties, schools of social services, departments of psychology and sociology train practitioners and research workers for careers relatively well-defined for a market far from being saturated. So, in 1967 the department of criminology started its three-year baccalaureate program for professional training of students specializing in the field of treatment of criminals and crime prevention. New sectors, mostly in the field of prevention, opened up; criminology in the schools whose objective is to re-instate into society, youths who are in conflict with school authorities or with justice for minors; guidance counselors in clubs for leisure-time activities where marginal characters, deviants, drug addicts, etc. conglomerate. The applied orientation of training and research in the department was ratified by its obtaining the status of School, and thus becoming the "School of Criminology" in February 1972.

PROFESSORS AND STUDENTS: At present nearly three hundred students attend courses scaled over six years of studies, including graduate and postgraduate programs. Seventeen full-time and twelve part-time professors ensure the teaching load. Internships are much encouraged in third year, and a close collaboration is maintained with institutions and organizations of social defense.

Relations with the Government and the Public

The first problem that comes to mind concerning relations with the government is that of the labor market; the same is true when it comes to the reaction of the public: Is the "criminologist" on the up-to-date profession lists kept by the civil service commission? Was any need expressed by senior officials responsible for the administration of justice as to the number or nature of "criminologists"? If brought forth, would these needs be classified as priorities by the planning office, the Treasury Board, or other qualified government organizations?

This is obviously a major obstacle for those who want to develop criminology as a profession or as an applied science. In fact, criminology is the product of prospective thinking that is an option concerning the probability of a certain type of evolution or change in a specific sector of public administration; an evolution made possible by some favorable changes in public thinking. This option, of course, is not shared by all and there are very legitimate doubts as to the future evaluation of these needs. The same observation holds true when it comes to the "desirability" of this evolution and the trend of public thinking gravitating in such a direction, should the occasion arise.

It was not by underestimating these difficulties that we conceived the strategy of contacts and actions to undertake. This strategy aimed at two objectives. The first was to give civil servants or intellectual workers, already at work, concrete and practical tools to improve their work. We are essentially concerned with personnel in treatment and in the administration of penitentiaries, in probation services, on parole boards and police forces, and with educators of alienated youths. The second objective was to widen the gap thus created by pointing out the necessity of raising the requirements for professional training of personnel in other categories. The creation of new types of experts, made necessary by the growth of new forms of delinquency, was raised later on.

Government services ended by assisting in these endeavors, having recognized the advantages to be reaped in the race towards the effectiveness and the "professionalization" characterizing the sector of services in post-industrialized societies. In fact, the "sciences" sector involves tremendous improvement; the higher level of the schooling of the population should benefit all services, including those which were previously at a disadvantage, as was the case with the administration of justice. To facilitate matters, bursaries were arranged for students preparing for careers in criminology; internships were organized with the active assistance of public services.

And that is where *public opinion* plays its role. For without an evolution of thought favorable to reforms in the field of justice, politicians would hesitate to approve such action—fearful and conservative by definition—on the part of the administration. Not only was it necessary to generate a change of ideas and of moral values in communities uncommonly conservative in English Canada as well as in French Canada (even more so in the latter's case), but one had to try for a bonus for reform, that is, to make it possible for a politician to reap some credit, should he declare himself in favor of reform.

SOCIETIES OF CRIMINOLOGY: These trends in thinking came into being, thanks to semiscientific, semisocially oriented societies called "Societies of Criminology" which brought together judges, lawyers, doctors, police, and penitentiary administrators, as well as personnel from these services and citizens concerned with social problems. All controversies which had aroused public opinion, organized crime, prostitution, armed robbery, architecture of penitentiaries etc., were discussed publicly and in depth by these societies. An attitude of tolerance, comprehension, indeed of mutual respect, was generated among the various professions, factions, groups of thought, as regards some basic themes which were on everyone's mind: making the penal system more humane, protecting society more effectively without infringing on the civic rights of individuals and, essentially, recognizing the fact that legal, police, penitentiary, and preventive functions are interdependent and complementary.

A new, daily incorporated, professional association has grouped all the graduates in criminology. Established to protect the common interests of its members, this association plays a role, by no means small, in the acceptance of criminology on the labor market.

GOVERNMENT COMMISSIONS OF ENQUIRY: Thanks to power-play politics in a parliamentary democracy, some political parties came to include reforms in the field of social defense in their platforms; this resulted among other things, in the creation of a Commission of Enquiry into the Administration of Criminal Justice in Quebec, on the provincial level, and in a Canadian Committee on Corrections in Ottawa, on the federal.

Professors of criminology acted as researchers and as scientific consultants in the two organizations entrusted with the preparation of a series of reforms of the entire system under their respective jurisdiction. The chairmen of these commissions and committees played a very important part in defining blueprints for reforms. These proposed reforms triggered productive public discussions which greatly contributed to the evolution of morals in favor of change. The conclusions and recommendations by these commissions of enquiry comprise a complete program of reforms for use by the government in the coming decades. They insist upon major contributions from universities, i.e. the field of training and research.

Conclusions

What conclusions are we to draw from this Canadian venture carried out in Montreal? Can this knowledge be extrapolated or exchanged? What does it owe to exceptional circumstances, to chance, to the action of people and groups peculiar to the milieu?

It is obvious that the unique historical experience is always the result of special men or groups encountering a specific situation. From their confrontation, from their action, emerges a reality which is inscribed in the history of a country or an institution. The experience I have analyzed, obviously falls in this category.

However, the same challenges could produce identical reactions; and the same social forces could cause similar phenomena. The error, by some sociological determinism, was to think that these ties were necessary; the fact that they are only probable, is already sufficient to set up a certain "science," that of "historical forecasting."

In Canada, the University of Ottawa and some universities in Toronto and Alberta have already followed our example.

We would like to submit the Canadian operation for testing

by comparative methods: The International Centre for Comparative Criminology, in collaboration with the International Society for Criminology, has the task of promoting similar methods all over the world, after adapting them to the special requirements of specific sociocultural contexts. This experiment, in progress for two years, is unfolding before our eyes. Eight years from now the time will be ripe for making the first balance sheet.

CHAPTER 13

CRIMINOLOGIST: THEORETICIAN
OR PRACTITIONER

—————— C. H. S. Jayewardene ——————

Professor Jayewardene is a member of the Department of Criminology, University of Ottawa, Ottawa, Canada.

W HO IS A CRIMINOLOGIST? Like most questions in criminology, this too is apparently one that defies answer. The difficulty appears to lie in the fact that those who call themselves criminologists today have had their training in a variety of disciplines, each with its own peculiar orientation. These orientations have been protected and maintained inviolate by an isolationism and an alienation which has made criminology a broadly and vaguely defined discipline into which anyone and everyone could facilely move, defying both definition and identification, training and orientation. This appears to be a major problem in criminology. The multiplicity of disciplines contributing to criminology have prevented criminology from having an identity of its own, its own scientific know-how, its own technology. It has made every criminologist, so to speak, unique, sharing with each other little more than a common title.

After a historical survey of the Canadian penal system, Szabo (1962) has contended that progress, slow at first, but inspired in recent times, could be retarded in the future by the absence of qualified staff capable of putting methods of reeducation into effect within the framework of penal institutions and under the system of supervised liberty. With a punitive philosophy all that was needed was custodial staff for whom no special training was deemed necessary. Protecting those outside from those inside, this staff had to identify themselves sufficiently with those outside and be capable of restraining those inside. With a rehabilitative orientation aimed at changing the situation of the inmate in a way presumed to be best for him, conditions changed. Persons with special skills were required (Mathieson, 1966).

An analysis of the papers presented at the fourth Canadian Congress of Criminology at Winnipeg in June 1963 forced Bertrand (1964) to conclude that the programs for training personnel in the field of delinquency and crime in Canada were characterized by inadequacies and pragmatism, lacking quality and efficacy. The primary deficiency appeared to be the inability to categorically state the recruitment qualifications—the type of training necessary for a given category of service. Part of this deficiency seemingly laid in the vagueness of the aims and goals of correctional institutions (Fornataro, 1963). As both Fornataro (1963) and Sinclair (1963) stress, the organization of a training program presupposed the existence of the institutions' authorized objectives expressed in clear unequivocal terms. The critical questions appeared to be "What is the purpose of the activity in which the officers are engaged?" "What kind of result is required?" and "What means are consistent with its attainment?" (Fornataro, 1963). It was only when these questions were answered that training became meaningful.

Even when these questions are answered the problem is unlikely to be resolved unless there are specific programs for the training of correctional personnel. When the training is done by some other discipline, however closely related it may be to Criminology, and however great its contribution to criminology may be, additional training is frequently necessary. The decadal directive of 1962 of the Social Work Council for the North American Continent made this position amply clear in the curriculum changes suggested so as to assist schools of Social Work to prepare students for the correctional field (Prigmore, 1963). The John Howard Society of Ontario felt it necessary to provide its employees, mainly social workers, with a more specific orientation, and they found that the staff training time and effort were of mutual benefit both for the agency and the staff (Ewald and Couse, 1963).

The multidisciplinary nature of criminology appears to pose a problem for the organization of specific training courses for correctional workers. Grygier (1962) has pointed out that there were two ways of circumventing this difficulty. There was the interdisciplinary approach which made use of and integrated the knowledge relating to crime and criminals in a multitude of disciplines. There was then, as opposed to this, the unified approach which looked upon criminology as a distinct entity developing its own methods and its own techniques, albeit from ones existing in other disciplines.

Contending that corrections required teamwork, Grygier's (1962) view was that criminology must develop as an interdisciplinary discipline, although this did not preclude the organization of centers of criminology for teaching and research purposes (Grygier, 1962b). Szabo, Frechette, and Ciale (1962) were in favor of criminology formation per se because the interdisciplinary approach, they concluded, referred to a collection of therapeutic and preventive methods as a subsidiary branch of psychiatry, social work, and clinical psychology. While this approach had practical value, it neglected the auxiliary disciplines of penology, criminalistics, and legal medicine which were the firmament of criminological thinking. Criminology must have its own specific concepts and standards as it was only then that a distinct profession of criminologists could be created.

A comprehensive study of the problem has been made by Markson and Hartman (1962 and 1963). They presented a detailed proposal for the establishment of an institute of criminology based on the results of enquiries into current thinking and practice in criminological teaching and research and upon the particular needs in Ontario as indicated by a survey of provincial universities, agencies, and government services. They identify the principal issues involved as (1) a pressing need for systematic research in the basic and practical problems of general criminology with such research being conducted on a multi- or interdisciplinary basis, the aim being to achieve a better understanding of crime and criminal behavior; (2) the need for teachers with adequate clinical and academic background; (3) the provision of objective data which is required for modification of the criminal law and of correctional practices; (4) public education and (5) advanced legal training for selected personnel holding critical positions in agencies which are engaged in the prevention and control of crime and the treatment of criminals.

The first year, they believed, should be spent in the learning of the basic disciplines and methods of criminology and criminological theory. This must be supplemented with field trips to appropriate agencies and institutions. The second year, they feel, should provide programs for students wishing to acquire competence in a particular aspect of criminology. In addition the students should participate in an on-going research or demonstration project or undertake a project of their own. Criminological teaching, in short, should be geared to the production of theory-conscious practitioners or practice-oriented theoreticians.

The multidisciplinary nature of criminology has been a matter of concern to American criminologists as well. They, however, appear to have approached the subject not from the point of view of practice as the Canadian criminologists have done, but from the point of view of theory. The viable future of criminology, it has been contended, was linked with the adoption of an interdisciplinary approach (Wolfgang, 1968) which would result in an integrated Criminology. Empirical data collected by independent disciplines and interpreted within the limited parameters of their orientation must be brought together in an analytic synthesis which would become, minimally, the combination of the parts and, maximally, a new perspective (Wolfgang and Ferracuti, 1967). The need for the adoption of an interdisciplinary approach to achieve integration is more or less universally acknowledged. This acknowledgment has not, however, resulted in unison of purpose. It appears to have generated the multifactor-single generalization controversy (Bianchi, 1958; Di Tullio, 1969; Ferracuti, 1971; Hartung, 1955; Mannheim, 1965; Radzinowicz, 1966; Schafer, 1969; Wolfgang and Ferracuti, 1967), stressing its focus essentially if not exclusively in the sphere of research and theory formulation.

This does not mean that no interest has been shown in the practitioner: It has. But then, the interest has been not in what he should do, in what training he should get, or in what contribution he could make to criminology. The interest has been in the theoretician-practitioner difference. This difference has been identified as essentially one of interest. The theoretician is seen as being essentially scientific. The producer of scientific knowhow, he utilizes the scientific method to establish relationships between events in his efforts to obtain a better overall understanding of the problem. He is interested in pluralities rather than in individuals, in types of cases rather than in individual cases, in similarities rather than in differences, in generalities rather than in specificities. It is he and he alone that can unravel the mysteries that shroud the criminogenic process. The practitioner, on the other hand, is seen as being essentially nonscientific. He may utilize the scientific knowhow. Yet, as his aim has been not the understanding of the overall phenomenon but the individual case he must do something about, he has been interested in individuals, not in pluralities—in the case, not in types of cases; in differences, not in similarities; in specificities, not in generalities (Hunt, 1951; Marx, 1956; Meehl, 1954; Trasler, 1962, 1964; Wilkins, 1968, 1969).

In Canada today there are three Centers of Criminology—in Montreal, in Ottawa and in Toronto. The School of Montreal was established in 1960 with a graduate program in criminology. Defining criminology as *"la science qui étudie le crime, le criminel et la victime afin d'établir les facteurs à l'origine du comportement antisocial et afin de trouver les meilleurs moyens de lutter contre ce comportement ainsi que les mesures aptes à la prevenir et les méthodes efficaces de resocialiser les délinquants et criminels,"* they concentrated on the production of practitioners well-versed in criminological theory, though, of course, the traditional research and theory formulation endeavors necessary for the development of a university department of good academic standing were not neglected (Université de Montreal, 1972-1973).

The Center in Toronto started a Master's program in criminology in 1971. The Center itself was established in 1963 for the purpose of taking "full advantage of, and coordinating the research work being done into various aspects bearing on the total field of criminology by existing disciplines in the University." In keeping with this aim, the teaching program of this school is "research oriented, integrated with existing and future research projects in the Center . . . intended to provide students with advanced study and supervised research experience." It is not intended to train practitioners who, it is contended, "simply require additional technical and vocational training of a kind obtainable through in-service training programs . . ." (University of Toronto, 1971-1972).

The graduate program of the University of Ottawa, started in 1968, was designed to train both theoreticians and practitioners with two parallel curricula having a common base. The parallel curricula were deemed necessary because the endeavors of the two were different and called for the possession of different skills; the common base deemed essential because the endeavors of the one were considered important for the endeavors of the other (University of Ottawa, 1972-1973). The development of the program at the University of Montreal, boasting now of baccalaureate, masters and doctoral programs, permitting specialization as a researcher and theoretician or as a practitioner, seems to endorse this view.

What approach an independent school of criminology should adopt in the teaching of its students is a question that has not yet been answered. What is now looked upon as the traditional method is the one that was adopted for instruction in criminology when criminology was taught as a specialty of some other discipline—concentration on theory and research. With criminology becoming a discipline in its own right, is this approach adequate? Schools outside Canada, that have demonstrated the autonomy of criminology, with programs of study ranging from the baccalaureate to the doctoral, adopt different methods.

At the University of California, the School of Criminology is "concerned with rational social policies for dealing with crime and criminals—policies that will help enlarge freedom and increase justice in society." Its teaching program is geared toward the attainment of this goal (University of California, 1970-1971). At the University of South Africa, the main aim is the "promotion of professional efficiency and vocational consciousness." Towards the achievement of this end, research and theory formulation is stressed but not without the recognition of the need for a clinical department actively engaged in the preinstitutional, institutional and postinstitutional care of prisoners where teachers could demonstrate how to do what, according to them, should be done (University of South Africa, 1967).

A curriculum symposium organized by the University of Ottawa (Sheppard, 1971) revealed the existence of three schools of thought, of three distinct and separate viewpoints in this connection. There were those who believed that primacy of place should be given to the training of researchers and theoreticians: according to them a school of criminology should not depart from the traditional. Then there were those who thought that the production of practitioners was the most important task: to them a school of criminology was essentially a trade school. Finally, there were those who insisted that what a school of criminology should do was to produce a criminologist with equal stress on research, theory and practice—a criminologist who could blossom out into a theoretician or a practitioner with equal facility.

Those who wanted primacy of place in teaching given to the training of researchers and theoreticians believed that the future of criminology, as a science, was dependent on the existence of a scientifically verified body of knowledge. Consequently, in their view, the prime aim of a school of criminology should be the training of persons who would aid in the production of this body of knowledge. Practitioners, they contended, should be given training, but at the present time only avocationally, to keep them aware of the developments in the field. Crime control and crime prevention, they felt, could be achieved through the efforts of practitioners only when a body of scientifically proven knowledge existed. Until then, the training of practitioners would be through faith rather than through science, with speculation rather than with fact. It would be a training that was not only wasteful but farcical as well.

Those who contended that the production of practitioners was the most important task believed that the future of criminology was dependent on the demonstration of its ability to deal with the problem at hand. What mattered, they contended, was not the soundness or the attractiveness of the theory but what the criminologist actually did to alleviate the existing problem. Theoreticians, they conceded, were necessary to provide the theoretical basis for programs of crime prevention and crime control. But, in the absence of such a basis, they asked, must nothing be done? A sound theoretical basis, they believed, could be produced not by the statistical manipulation of variables, but by the alteration and manipulation of factors that have been considered criminogenic. This task only the practitioner could perform.

Those who stressed the equal importance of theory and practice believed that the essential function of theory was to guide practice and the essential function of practice was to refine and reformulate theory. To them, practice without the support of theory was wasteful and theory without the support of practice was speculative. The practitioner-theoretician dichotomy, they contended, has been the bane of criminology, for it has deprived criminology of the use of the most important tool of the scientific method—experimentation. Schools of criminology, consequently, must seek to produce people who can translate theory into practice and utilize practice in the formulation of theory, even though some may concentrate on the one and some on the other.

It could perhaps be argued that the practitioner-theoretician difference is in reality a very superficial difference having its roots in the multidisciplinary nature of criminology, which is bound to disappear when criminology becomes an integrated entity with a body of knowledge of its own. Sixteenth and seventeenth century medicine, which did not possess a body of scientifically proven knowledge, was plagued with the distinction made between the theoretician and the practitioner, supported by the belief that involvement in research and theory formulation offered greater hope for the discipline and conferred greater status on the individual than did practice (Lueth, 1971). Even today there is necessarily in every field of knowledge an essential difference between the theoretician and the practitioner. But, in most of them the difference has been minimized. Though the theoretician concentrates on adding to the body of knowledge and the practitioner draws on it, the two do not see themselves in mutually exclusive positions. They seem to be kept together by a "common professional training, a common methodological ground and a status unity" (Wolfgang and Ferracuti, 1967). These common factors exist, however, because the endeavors of the one have an impact on the endeavors of the other. The practitioner's problems of today are the theoretician's problems of tomorrow and the theoretician's success of today is the practitioner's success of tomorrow. The one is essential for the existence of the other; the one is an essential part of the other. Without the practitioner, the theoretician's work would be an academic exercise and, without the theoretician, the practitioner's work would be a blind adventure.

In criminology, unfortunately, this is not the case. Not only have the theoretician and the practitioner come into criminology with different orientations, their spheres of operation also have been different. The theoretician has worked on one side of the legal machinery—the societal agency entrusted with the labelling of individuals as criminal or delinquent. The practitioner has worked on the other. While the theoretician has been mainly concerned with why the label has been put on, why an individual has become a criminal, the practitioner has been concerned with how to remove the label, how to rehabilitate the criminal and reintegrate him into society. Though there is an essential link between the two, they are not necessarily the obverse and reverse sides of the same coin. Consequently, the endeavors of the one have little or no meaning for the endeavors of the other. The practitioner does not, because he cannot, convert the success of the theoretician into his own success. The theoretician does not, because he need not, make the problems of the practitioner his own.

True enough the full understanding of the problem is an essential prerequisite for its control. But the building up of a body of scientific knowledge is only the means to the achievement of the goal of scientific study—the human control of the phenomenon subjected to investigation. In discussing the relationship between knowledge and control, between theory and practice, Dewey (1931) contended that it was a complete error to suppose that efforts at social control depend upon the prior existence of a social science. He went further to contend that the building up of a social science was dependent upon putting social planning into effect. In the process imperfect and even wrong hypotheses were acted upon, but these brought to light significant phenomena which made improved ideas and improved experimentations capable of leading finally to knowledge and control by the application of the knowledge gained.

Such, however, is only possible with the integration of theory and practice as achieved in medicine. Success in the research and theoretical endeavors of medicine came when practice, with speculation based on the meager existing knowledge, was utilized to ensure, enrich and enlarge that knowledge. It came as a result of a joint venture in which theoretician and practitioner, participating as equal partners, sought to secure the most efficient means for the attainment of a common goal. It was a venture in which the theoretician, through practice, demonstrated the value of his theory and the practitioner, through theory, demonstrated the value of his technique (Lueth, 1971). The joint venture did even more. The unique case approach of the practitioner, viewed today as a veritable obstacle to scientific endeavor in criminology, was recognized as having methodological utility for research and theory formulation. Generalizations were not attempted from the individual case but the individual case was used to naturally define and refine the unit of study (MacMahon, Pugh and Ipsen, 1960). With this, of course, research and theory formulation became less ambitious. The understanding of the total phenomenon could not be sought in one broad sweep: it had to come through the summation of the understanding of the multitude of segments that comprised the total phenomenon.

All this does not mean that researchers and theoreticians in criminology have ignored practice completely. Studies have been made of correctional institutions in order to improve our knowledge of what goes on in them (Clemmer, 1940; Cloward, Cressey, Grosser, McCleery, Ohlin, Sykes and Messinger, 1960; Cressey, 1961; Schrag, 1954; Sykes, 1958; Polsky, 1962; Ward and Kassebaun, 1964). Correctional processes and treatment procedures have been evaluated (Bailey, 1966; England, 1955; Glaser, 1964; Grygier, 1965; Grygier, Guarino, Nease and Sakunicz, 1968; McCorkle, 1952; Zalba, 1967), and experiments in crime control and crime prevention have been attempted (Crawford, Malamud and Dumpson, 1950; Empey and Lubeck, 1971; Kassebaum, Ward and Wilner, 1971; Miller, 1962; Meyer, Borgatta and Jonas, 1965; Powers and Witmer, 1951; Weeks, 1958). All, however, have succeeded in revealing to the practitioner not what should be done but what should not. This, perhaps, is all that can be achieved at the present moment but then, it will continue to remain all that can be achieved until the theoretician becomes practice-oriented and the practitioner becomes theory-conscious.

In a school of criminology where criminology is viewed as an integrated discipline, who should be trained is a real problem. If criminology will not train its own researchers and theoreticians nobody will. Unfortunately this is not the same as far as practitioners are concerned. If criminology will not train its practitioners somebody else certainly will. Then the practitioner will come into criminology with tools that do not permit him to utilize the theory that the theoretician has so meticulously developed, theory he developed without stopping to ask the relevant question, "Knowledge for what?" In criminology the integration of theory and practice is as great a need as the interdisciplinary integration of its theory. When knowledge does not exist, the situation may be described as pathetic. Even more pathetic is the situation where knowledge exists and is not used. But when knowledge exists and cannot be used, the situation is more than pathetic—it is a tragedy, in the ancient Greek sense of the word. What is criminology—a pure science or an applied science? Who is a criminologist—a theoretician or a practitioner? These are questions that must be answered.

REFERENCES

Bailey, W. C.: Correctional outcome: An evaluation of 100 reports. *J Crim Law Criminal, 57*:153-1960, 1966.

Bertrand, M. A.: Les Programmes de formation du personnel dans le domain criminologie au Canada. *Can J Correct, 6*:308-319, 1964.

Bianchi, H.: *Position and Subject Matter of Criminology.* Amsterdam, North-Holland Publishing Company, 1956.

Clemner, D.: *The Prison Community.* New York, Rinehart, 1958.

Cloward, R. A., Cressey, D. R., Grosser, G. H., McCleery, R., Ohlin, L. E., Sykes, G. M. and Messinger, S. L.: *Theoretical Studies in Social Organization of the Prison.* New York, Social Science Research Council, 1960.

Crawford, P., Malamud, D. I. and Dumpson, J. R.: *Working with Teenage Gangs.* New York, Welfare Council of New York City, 1950.

Cressey, D. R.: *The Prison: Studies in Institutional Organization and Change.* New York, Holt, Rinehart and Winston, 1961.

Dewey, J.: Social science and social control. *New Republic, 67*:276-277, 1931.

DiTullio, B.: *Horizons of Clinical Criminology.* New York, New York University Criminal Law Education and Research Center, 1969.

Empey, L. T. and Lubeck, S. G.: *The Silver Lake Experiment. Testing Delinquency Theory and Community Intervention.* 1971.

England, R. W.: A study of postprobation recidivism among five hundred federal offenders. *Fed Probation, 19*:10-16, 1955.

Eward, F. E. A. and Couse, A. K.: Staff training in the John Howard Society of Ontario. *Can J Correct, 5*:347-353, 1963.

Ferracuti, F.: *Coordination of Interdisciplinary Research in Crominology.* (Rome, United Nations Social Defence Research Institute), 1971.

Fornataro, J. V.: What are the staff training problems for Canadian prisons. *Can J Correct, 5*:292-301, 1963.

Glaser, D.: *The Effectiveness of a Prison and Parole System.* Indianapolis, Bobbs-Merrill, 1964.

Grygier, T.: Education for correctional workers. A survey of needs and resources. *Can J Correct, 4*:347-353, 1962.

———: *The Teaching of Criminology as a Part of the Curriculum of a Department of Psychology.* Paper presented at the 3rd Research Conference on Crime and Delinquency, Montreal, 1962.

———: *Social Adjustment, Personality and Behaviour in Training Schools in Ontario.* University of Toronto School of Social Work, 1965.

Grygier, T., Guarino, M., Nease, B. and Sakowicz, L.: Social interaction in small units: new methods of treatment and its evaluation. *Can J Correct, 10*:252-260, 1968.

Hartung, F. G.: Methodological assumption in a social-psychological theory of criminality. *J Crim Law Criminol, 45:*652-661, 1955.

Hunt, W. A.: Clinical psychology—science or superstition. *Am Psychol, 6:* 683-687, 1951.

Kassebaum, G., Ward, D. A. and Wilner, D. M.: *Prison Treatment and Parole Survival: An Empirical Assessment.* 1971.

Lueth, P.: *Lehren und Lernen in der Medèzin.* Stuttgart, Georg. Thieme Verlag, 1971.

MacMahon, B., Pugh, T. F. and Ipsen, J.: *Epidemiologic Methods.* Boston, Little, Brown and Co., 1960.

Mannheim, H.: *Comparative Criminology.* London, Routledge and Kegan Paul, 1965.

Markson, E. P. and Hartman, V.: Function and Organization of a Model Institute of Criminology. Paper presented at the 3rd Research Conference on Crime and Delinquency, Montreal, 1962.

————: Function and organization of a model institute of criminology. *Can J Correct, 5:*11-27, 1963.

Marx, M. H.: Sources of confusion in attitudes toward clinical theory. *J Gen Psychol, 55:*19-20, 1956.

Mathieson, T.: The sociology of prisons: Problems for future research. *Br J Sociol, 17:*360-399, 1966.

Meehl, P. E.: *Clinical vs. Statistical Prediction.* Minneapolis, University of Minnesota Press, 1954.

McCorkle, L. W.: Group therapy in the treatment of offenders. *Fed Probation, 16:*22-27, 1952.

Meyer, H. J., Borgatta, E. F. and Jones, W. C.: *Girls at Vocational High. An Experiment in Social Work Intervention.* New York, Russel Sage Foundation), 1965.

Miller, W. B.: The impact of a total community delinquency control project. *Soc Prob, 10:*188-191, 1962.

Polsky, H. W.: *Cottage Six.* New York, Russel Sage Foundation, 1962.

Powers, E. and Sitmer, H.: *An Experiment in the Prevention of Delinquency.* New York, Columbia University Press, 1951.

Prigmore, C. S.: Correction and social work. The impact of the 1962 curriculum policy statement. *Crime Delinq, 9:*185-188, 1963.

Radzinowicz, L.: *Ideology and Crime.* London, Heinemann Educational Books, 1966.

Schafer, S.: *Theories in Criminology.* New York, Random House, 1969.

Schrag, C.: Leadership among prison inmates. *Am Sociol Rev, 19:*37-42, 1954.

Sheppard, C. S.: *Curriculum Symposium.* University of Ottawa Center of Criminology, 1971.

Sinclair, D.: In service training and the goals of institutional treatment. *Can J Correct, 5:*97-109, 1963.

Sykes, G. H.: *The Society of Captives.* Princeton, Princeton University Press, 1958.

Szabo, D.: Evolution et etat present du systeme judiciare penitentiare et policier du Canada. *Rev Droit pen Criminol, 43:*135-149, 1962.

Szabo, D., Frechette, Mr. and Cicele, J.: A note on the teaching of criminology. A reply to Dr. T. Grygier. *Can J Correct, 4:*205-209, 1963.

Trasler, G.: *The Explanation of Criminality.* London, Routleded and Kegan Paul, 1962.

————: Strategic problems in the study of criminal behavior. *Br J Criminol, 4:*422-442, 1962.

Université de Montreal: *Ecole de Criminologie.* Université de Montreal Faculté des Arts et des Sciences, 1972-73.

University of California: *School of Criminology,* University of California Berkeley, 1970-71.

University of Ottawa: *Criminology,* University of Ottawa Graduate Studies 1972-73.

University of South Africa: *Department of Criminology,* University of South Africa Department of Criminology, 1967.

University of Toronto: *Center of Criminology,* University of Toronto Center of Criminology, 1971-72.

Ward, D. A. and Kassebaum, G. G.: Homosexuality: A mode of adaptation in a prison for women. *Soc Prob, 12:*159-177, 1964.

Weeks, H. A.: *Youthful Offenders at Highfields.* Ann Arbor, University of Michigan Press, 1958.

Wilkins, L. T.: The concept of cause in criminology. *Issues Criminol, 3:*147-166, 1968.

————: *Evaluation of Penal Measures.* New York, Random House, 1969.

Wolfgang, M. E.: The viable future of criminology. In Szabo, D.: *Criminology in Action.* Montreal, La Presse de l' Université, 1968.

Wolfgang, M. E. and Ferracuti, F.: *The Subculture of Violence.* London, Tavistock Publications, 1967.

Zalba, S. R.: Work release—A two-pronged effort. *Crime Delinq, 13:*506-512, 1967.

CHAPTER 14

THE CRIMINOLOGY CENTER—A VIABLE MODEL FOR KNOWLEDGE IMPACT IN AREAS OF DISPERSED POPULATION

ROMINE R. DEMING, PH.D.

Professor Deming is Director, UMD Criminology Center School of Social Work, University of Minnesota, Duluth, Minnesota.

INTRODUCTION

THIS PAPER DEALS with the problem of providing knowledge for criminal justice administration and the promotion of concerted effort in areas of dispersed population. It suggests a model for a delivery system which provides criminological information and promotes cooperation between the public, criminal justice agencies, and the university. This paper presents the results of implementing a specific model in a given region which has a dispersed population. Lastly, it presents suggestions for the implementation of this model in other geographical regions.

STATEMENT OF THE PROBLEM

The crime rate is high in areas of dense population or urban areas. However, it is also very high in areas of dispersed population or rural areas. In addition, the crime rate is increasing in areas of dispersed population. In areas with the greatest dispersed population there was an increase of 8 percent in the first quarter of 1972.

There are more resources in areas of dense population. The resources available to areas of dispersed population are too meager or nonexistent. There is little in the *natural evolution* of areas with dispersed population to increase criminal justice resources and enhance criminal justice administration.

Two resources which are of primary importance to criminal

144

justice are knowledge and concerted effort. These resources are in many cases sufficient to solve many of the criminal justice problems. These resources serve as catalysts to produce other resources. Lastly, these resources improve the efficient use of all resources.

Although the Omnibus Crime Control and Safe Streets Act of 1968 has provided an increase in funds to criminal justice in the United States, it has had little benefit for areas of dispersed population. This is especially the case in terms of development and communication of knowledge. Research and education are still oriented to and located in densely populated areas. There are 850 university or college criminal justice programs in the United States. Most are confined to an academic or teaching role. Some also include a role of research, usually having a national focus. Few are committed to full knowledge impact for a particular area. This division of labor and specialization is perhaps justifiable in densely populated areas with sufficient informational resources, but it cannot be justified in areas of dispersed population.

In regards to enhancing concerted effort, in many cases the Act has had the opposite effect. In too many cases, the meager resources provided by the Act has done little more than increase the conflict already existing in the fragmented criminal justice process. It has detracted from, rather than promoted, systemness.

This paper then is addressed to the problem of enhancing criminal justice in areas of dispersed population through knowledge impact and the promotion of concerted effort.

A THEORETICAL MODEL OF A CRIMINOLOGY CENTER

It is felt that the best unit to solve the problem is a criminology center. A criminology center is seen in this paper as a university-based unit established on joint funding between the university and the region or the university and the state. Regional and state funding should be attained through sources independent of the university. The true role of the criminology center model should be research, public service and teaching.

The following model was essentially developed from higher

education theory and the needs of criminal justice in areas of dispersed population. It was established independent of the setting in which it was tested. The criteria used for site selection was the degree of commitment to a concerted effort for the enhancement of criminal justice. The commitment of the public, criminal justice agencies and the university of many proposed sites were assessed. In short, the site with the greatest appreciation and commitment to the model was selected. Incidentally, the site that was selected was not the highest bidder in monetary terms. The degree of concerted effort was demonstrated, among other means, by joint funding between the Regional Crime Council and the university.

Assumptions

The following assumptions are the basis for the model:
1. The university exists to serve the people of the region, the state and the nation.
2. The university has the primary responsibility to develop, accumulate and communicate knowledge to students, governmental agencies and the public.
3. The university should develop, accumulate and communicate knowledge pertinent to criminal justice agencies i.e., crime prevention, law enforcement, judicial agencies and corrections.
4. There is a national need for knowledgeable personnel to fill staff positions in criminal justice and criminology.
5. The university education should focus on developing analytical, problem-solving ability, not on technical knowledge or skills.
6. The university should provide a relevant curriculum for interested students so they may fill these positions.

Objective

The acceptance of these assumptions logically results in the formulation of the following objective for the Criminology Center: *The objective of the Criminology Center is to develop, collect and communicate knowledge relevant to crime causation, its prevention, and control.*

Accepting this objective permits breaking the ivory tower bonds to truly serve the geographical region in which the Criminology Center is located. It permits the drawing of resources from within the university, the region and the nation to solve regional criminal justice problems and to educate. The Center serves all, i.e. the public, the students and the criminal justice agencies of the area. It is not set apart from the region, but is a part of the region.

In addition, the objective promotes systemic linkage between the university and the region. It promotes interaction between students and criminal justice agencies. Lastly, it promotes interaction and systemic linkage between the various criminal justice agencies within the region.

The university's search for objective knowledge provides a neutral ground to explore and resolve differences. The university staff are well suited to the role of mediators of conflicts between groups. The Criminology Center, through its objectives, can bring conflicting groups together to gain concerted effort in addition to developing, accumulating and communicating knowledge.

Missions

In analyzing the objective, four component missions are crystalized. They are: research, career preparation, criminal justice planning and public education. By being aware of the component missions, a plan consciously derived can be employed to accomplish as many missions as possible with one set of resources. This permits efficient use of resources. An example of this can be found in the evaluation of attitudinal change of adjudicated delinquents in a group counseling program of a probation department. Students become aware of the problems of the agency, learn about research and become acquainted with attitudes of delinquents. The agency's staff benefit by being exposed to novel ideas of students and Criminology Center staff, by gaining knowledge from research results and by enhancing their public image as a progressive agency. The Criminology Center benefits by acquiring a consumer for its service and by gaining information to communicate regionally, nationally and internationally.

The public benefits by gaining knowledge of its agency's accomplishments, and by gaining a more efficient probation department.

The Setting

Northeastern Minnesota was selected as the site for the experiment of a Criminology Center based on the above model. This region was the first out-state planning region in Minnesota to organize. It consists of seven counties with a total area of 17,950 square miles. One of these counties is the largest county east of the Mississippi River. The three largest counties are also the three largest counties in the state. Northeastern Minnesota is one of the largest planning regions in the United States. The region is larger than nine states; in fact, it is almost twice the size of the larger of these states. It is larger than five of these nine states put together.

In terms of population, it has a total population of 329,603 of which almost one third, 100,578, live in Duluth. Subtracting the land area and population of Duluth from the region, there are approximately thirteen people per square mile or a density index of 12.80 for the remainder of the region.

In terms of higher education, there is one public university, the University of Minnesota, Duluth, with 5,000 students; one private college; and five junior colleges in this region.

In terms of criminal justice, there are six federal, two state, seven county, and thirty-four municipal law enforcement agencies. There are two judicial districts, seven juvenile courts, six county courts, fourteen municipal courts, seven county attorney offices and two public defender offices. There are two correctional field service agencies, a juvenile detention center and a regional corrections center. Lastly, there are ninety agencies involved in crime and delinquency prevention.

This, then, is Northeastern Minnesota, the site selected. It was an ideal site in terms of the problems of administering criminal justice in a region of dispersed population. This region is typical of many states and regions of states throughout the nation.

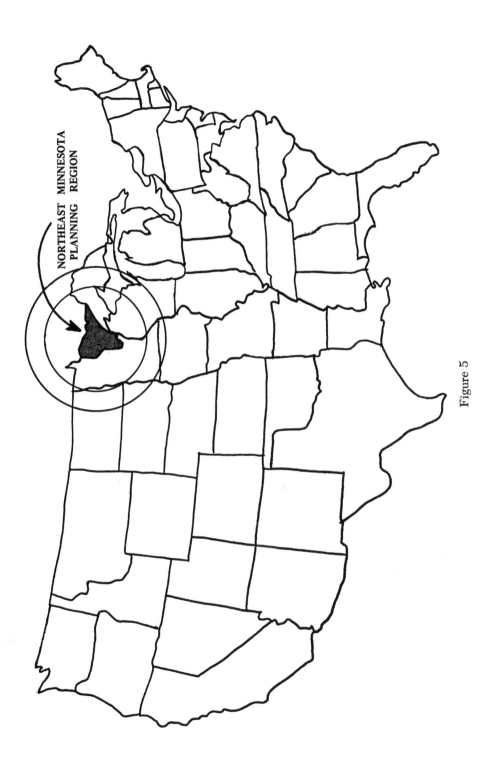

NORTHEAST MINNESOTA PLANNING REGION

Figure 5

KNOWLEDGE IMPACT OF THE CRIMINOLOGY CENTER

It is best to illustrate the impact of the Center by cataloging the accomplishments made by the UMD Criminology Center over the past three years. The accomplishments are presented under the most appropriate mission label. The reader will recognize that a given accomplishment may contribute to one or more other missions. Of course, this is desirable for efficient use of resources. There are obviously many implicit accomplishments that cannot be elaborated on here for lack of space.

Before proceeding, however, there are certain principles which were fundamental in executing the missions. The primary principle was to exploit the legitimate invitations for the Center to enter other systems. The involvement in the other systems permitted encouragement for the development and use of knowledge and the promotion of a concerted effort with those systems. The principle of flexible priorities was heavily stressed. Whichever mission seemed to have the greatest priority at any given period of time was emphasized, thus increasing the efficiency of resource application. The principle of flexibility of resources was also stressed. Every effort was made not to lock in resources which would have a tendency to exist for periods longer than they were needed. Lastly, the principle of balance between need and growth was stressed. Every effort was made to avoid building an empire of resources and then locating the problem to focus them on. Applying these principles resulted in the following accomplishments by the UMD Criminology Center for Northeastern Minnesota.

RESEARCH

Reports

"The Drunkenness Offender of Duluth"

"Northeastern Minnesota Criminal Justice Profile"

"Northeastern Minnesota Adult Detention and Short-Term Corrections"

"Northeastern Minnesota Community Attitudes of Law Enforcement"

"Demographic Data of Northeastern Minnesota for Social Development?"

CRIMINAL JUSTICE PLANNING

System Development

Regional Crime Council

Duluth Municipal Probation Service

St. Louis County Work Farm

Duluth Police-Community Relations Unit

Northeast Regional Corrections Center

Program Evaluation

Duluth Municipal Probation Service

St. Louis County Work Farm

Duluth Police-Community Relations Unit

Training Programs

Psychology for Law Enforcement Officers

Regional Institute in Police-Community Relations

Human Relations Course in Recruit School

Correctional Innovation

Law Enforcement Consolidation

General Consultation

Regional Crime Council and its four task forces

Duluth Police Department

St. Croix Youth Camp

Duluth Municipal Court

St. Louis County Probation Department

Minnesota Crime Commission

Duluth Office of Research and Planning

Nett Lake Indian Reservation

Silver Bay Police Department

CAREER PREPARATION

Academic Program Development

University of Minnesota, Duluth, Department of Sociology-Anthropology

Criminology Curriculum

School of Social Work

Criminal Justice Planning Curriculum

    Mesabi State Junior College
      Law Enforcement Curriculum
    Hibbing State Junior College
      Law Enforcement Curriculum
Teaching
    University of Minnesota, Duluth
      Criminology Curriculum, a fifty-one credit program
    Mesabi State Junior College
      Law Enforcement, a twenty-five credit program
Educational Aids
    Produced 23, forty-five minute, video-taped, simulated correctional field trips of institutions in Minnesota, Iowa, Wisconsin and two federal institutions

PUBLIC EDUCATION
    Television and Newspaper Releases
    Public Presentations
    Course Introduction to Criminal Justice
    General Consultation to Various Groups

In terms of organization, the advisory board is itself a major vehicle for promoting intraregional cooperation and concerted effort. The UMD Criminology Center's advisory board is composed of the following encumbents:

UMD Assistant Provost (Chairman);
Vice-Provost for Academic Administration;
Director, School of Social Work;
Chairman of Division, Social Sciences;
Head of the Department of Sociology-Anthropology;
Associate Professor of the Department of Political Science;
Assistant Financial Aids Coordinator;
Chairman, Sociology Club;
President, Mesabi State Junior College;
Chairman, Regional Criminal Justice Committee;
Supervisor, Regional Office of the Department of Corrections;
Chief of the Duluth Police Department;
Juvenile Court Judge;
St. Louis County Chief Probation Officer;
Editor, *Duluth News Tribune.*

The UMD Criminology staff has increased from one person to six associates within a period of three years. It accomplished research tasks that were previously nonexistent. In terms of career preparation, it developed and serviced the Criminology curriculum which increased from three credits to fifty-one credits, servicing 125 students per year at the University of Minnesota, Duluth. It developed a twenty-five-credit curricula at two junior colleges and serviced one junior college, none of which were in existence three years ago. Not only was it able to provide an extensive knowledge impact, but was able to foster concerted effort within criminal justice administration and between students and criminal justice, the university faculty and criminal justice, and these units with the public. It is doubtful that any of this could exist without the Criminology Center model.

This is not to imply that there were no problems. Much was learned as a result of implementation of the model. We hope that others can profit by our problems and experiences.

SUGGESTIONS

The following suggestions are stressed. Of foremost importance is the commitment of the region to the university as an educational center for that region or state. It is paramount that the university, criminal justice agencies and the public accept the assumptions and the resulting objectives of the Center. Secondly, the Criminology Center should be subsidized through both university funds and extra-university funds. It is best that both funding resources provide a minimum of sustaining operational money. This could be provided by a share of the university budget plus a general revenue contribution to the Center. In lieu of and also in addition to sustaining funding, local units of government and criminal justice agencies can purchase consulting services from the Criminology Center in order that there may be a joint university and community financial responsibility. Thirdly and consistant with the previous two suggestions is that an advisory board be composed of university representatives, criminal justice agency administrators and citizens representing the public.

In some regions and states, the Regional Crime Council or

State Crime Commission can serve as an advisory board. It is important that the required mix of people be contained in those councils or commissions if they are to be used successfully. It is important that the advisory board have an important input in policy decisions. Lastly, it is suggested that a core staff be appointed. A minimum of two plus a clerical staff is necessary. The staff should be committed to the Criminology Center Model and committed to providing a service for the region or the state. It is suggested that one staff member, at least, have a behavioral science emphasis in his criminal justice background. To reemphasize, all involved must be committed to the legitimate invasion of the Criminology Center into regional systems.

Summary

This paper was concerned with the problem of providing a knowledge impact in areas of dispersed population and the promotion of concerted effort for the solution of criminal justice problems. It presented a simple theoretical model to accomplish this. It discussed the application of this model to a particular experimental site. It presented the accomplishments of this particular model in one specific location. Lastly, it stressed a few general mechanical suggestions for the establishment of criminology centers for maximum knowledge impact in areas of dispersed population.

CHAPTER 15

CRIMINOLOGY AS A SOCIAL SCIENCE: PERSPECTIVES FOR TEACHING AND RESEARCH

——————————JAIME TORO CALDER——————————

Professor Calder is a member of the Social Science Research Center, University of Puerto Rico, Rio Piedras Campus, Puerto Rico. Professor Calder is also a member of the Executive Committee of the American Society of Criminology.

A S SUGGESTED BY THE TITLE of this paper, we aim at exposing some ideas—some new and others already known—on the eternally controversial topics: What is the proper field of study of criminology? What is the present state of criminology? Does contemporary criminology correspond to contemporary social needs? What is the perspective for contemporary teaching and research based on present social reality? As these questionings suggest, we consider that there is ample margin for pondering and evaluative examination, product of the historical moment in the development of criminology. We understand that contemporary criminology is undergoing a crucial stage in its history, for either the perspective for teaching and research is redefined and extended or it runs the risk of sinking in stagnation. This is the main topic of this paper.

Having expressed the frame of reference, it is obligatory to start this exposition with some comments on the field proper of action for criminology as a scientific discipline. This topic includes wide areas of discrepancies manifested in books on the subject, but varying in accordance with the interest and background of the authors. Nevertheless, the dynamic production which this field accumulates in the U.S.A. expresses experiences and knowledge under those definitions offered in multiple textbooks on the subject, among them, Sutherland and Cressey

(1970) are quoted: "Criminology is the body of knowledge regarding crime as a social phenomenon. It includes within its scope the processes of making laws, of breaking laws, and of reacting toward the breaking of laws."

Later on, the scope of the study of the subject is defined as follows: "Criminology consists of three principal divisions, as follows: (a) the sociology of law, which is an attempt at scientific analysis of the conditions under which criminal laws develop and which is seldom included in general books on criminology; (b) criminal etiology, which is an attempt at scientific analysis of the causes of crime; and (c) penology, which is concerned with the control of crime."

Objectives of criminology are specified as follows: "The objective of criminology is the development of a body of general and verified principles and of other types of knowledge regarding this process of law, crime, and treatment or prevention."

In general, the delimitation and contents expressed in these quotations correspond to the position of the discipline of criminology in the U.S.A. where the great majority of the criminologists are formed in the field of the social sciences, especially Sociology, and receive a rigorous training not only on theory of deviant behavior, but also in the methodology of science and research techniques. This has facilitated an intense research activity and an ample literary production in the field of criminology. When this effort for the acquisition of knowledge of the social phenomenon of criminal behavior and the social reactions to the same is accumulated objectively, data gathered using adequate instruments and techniques analyzed with the corresponding systematic rigidity, significant knowledge is generated attaining scientific quality and category. From this experience we have gathered a vast production that justifies the statement that criminology has grouped enough scientific knowledge to attain the category of an autonomous and separate discipline. At the same time, it is correct to consider it as a scientific discipline occupying a solid place among the disciplines that study human behavior.

There is no need for a detailed account of the accomplishments of criminological research in which instruments of clinical analysis, case studies of sociological or psychological approaches, of statistical techniques, etc., have been employed. These have encompassed diverse topics and approaches from the biological deterministic to biopsychological approaches, to eclectic and multifacetic approaches—all of them of a positivistic orientation. Recent attempts to relate social structures and their consequences in terms of social injustice and the failure of the society's instrumentalities to deal effectively with human demands and its criminological consequences have also been challenged by criminological research.

The accomplishments of criminology during the last seventy-five years establish a base to conclude that criminology deserves a position among the scientific disciplines of human behavior and its importance as a separate and autonomous scientific field of study of man. At the same time, we should recognize that criminology is related to other fields of study. Human behavior being its subject matter, it cannot escape the biological-physiological and social-cultural nature of being human without denying that the alternatives to explain criminal behavior through deterministic or multiphasetic approaches has failed. The exclusively positivistic character of human nature limits the human being in his search for an explanation of criminal behavior.

Criminology, a scientific discipline, actually needs revitalization of research and teaching by new approaches and scopes of problems. Positivism, the legal analytical approach, and a multi-faceted sociological approach have attained a well-deserved place in the history of criminology, but do not constitute the final page in its knowledge. We have to confess that these efforts and accomplishments were left behind in the accelerated change of our society.

Another interesting question is posed when we ask ourselves the question, "Should the criminologist be a researcher or a practitioner of criminology?" When expressed in that way a difficult dichotomy arises. In reality, we should not think of a criminologist taking the purist position of a researcher exclusively, but recognize that he has the social responsibility of sharing both his teaching and understanding of social phenomenon with society. This participation should prevent misinterpretations of his conceptions and theories. What we are really establishing is that our society needs the full benefit of the scarce resources available, and that the criminologist cannot hide from this responsibility by claiming a purist position. A criminologist, 1972-style, has to satisfy a social need by his contribution to the theoretical, to the empirical, and to the academic world. This triple role is an exigence for our changing society and its consequent complexity and problems.

The 60's abounded with evidence most revealing of the need to revitalize the criminological perspectives, its activities in research and in teaching. The spout of collective protests demanding a major participation and social justice, the questioning of the establishment and social instruments of justice, denotes the need to reorient criminological research and teaching to other aims. It seems that the new society, product of the social demographic economic phenomenon of urban industrial life, creates new situations, new demands, new dimensions and the need for new understanding that contemporary criminology cannot handle. The well-known principle that to be able to deal with problems one has to be familiar with its nature and extent, certainly is not true for contemporary criminology. The acceptance of this reality should be the pivot on which the inspiration and stimulus for the search of new criminologic horizons rests.

In the same manner, it is convenient to mention the importance of reuniting the efforts of different disciplines associated to the study of criminal behavior, such as penal law, medicine, psychology, anthropology, sociology, etc., to prevent unnecessary speculation on scientific criminological knowledge. This point of view has been mentioned previously by some authors. In my own country, where recently I was asked to talk to the Judiciary Penal Commission of the State Legislature on a bill for a new penal code for Puerto Rico, I manifested that the position on Public Safety that was under examination was not clear in its provisions. It was short of the scientific criminological knowledge now in existence, and was far from the cultural and historical reality of our society. Unfortunately, the situation is not an exception, but a common experience. This example should be enough to establish the need in the field of the study and research in criminology to unite the efforts and knowledge of all disciplines allied to the phenomenon in order to be able to have a real advancement in theoretical knowledge and its empirical application for social action.

We have already mentioned that positivistic approaches—either biological deterministic nature, psychological determinism, eclectic or multiphacetic—have been limited in explaining criminal behavior and in addition, as foundation for positive social action. The introduction of the notion of the importance of the social system in the formation of human behavior, and the special reference to the social structure—for this is the stage that limits the human being in its social formative experience—has been recently initiated. This is a promising approach, both for empirical research and for its theoretical and practical consequences. These have been demonstrated, first at the theoretical levels by contributions of Merton (1938), Becker (1963), Kitsuse (1962), Erikson (1962), and others; and second, by Cohen (1955), Miller (1958), Bordua (1961), Cloward and Ohlin (1960), and others in criminological research. The problem with this new current is the unfairness with the contribution: we have not been speaking of true sociological theories, but of observations on the phenomenon that allows for some conceptions and accounts of the same but not for substantive theories.

A change of emphasis to a true sociological one would open new horizons to criminological research problems and would demand new approaches contents for the teaching experience. As an example of enrichment of the research horizons, let me mention the new problematic arising from the administration of justice. Traditionally, a description of the system would be enough, and an understanding of the system would be taken for granted. A new approach will examine its philosophy and its instrumentation, and will pose the following questions: Does it really satisfy the needs of our society? Does it comply with and ensure justice in society? If it fails in its mission, to what extent does it negatively affect the social interest of the members of that society? To what extent does it act as a criminogenic agent? What sectors of society receive the impact?

A similar consequence results in the teaching of criminology when we emphasize an understanding of the social system and its effect on human behavior as the framework of the problem to be examined and understood. This is the challenge we face, and with imagination and creativity we must enrich everything for the benefit of the advancement of criminology as a social science.

REFERENCES

Becker, H. C.: *The Outsiders.* 1963.

Bordua, D. J.: Delinquent subcultures: Sociological interpretations of gang delinquency. *Ann Am Acad Politic Soc Sci, 338:*119-136, 1961.

Cloward, R. A. and Ohlin, L. E.: *Delinquency and Opportunity: A Theory of Delinquent Gangs.* 1960.

Cohen, A. K.: *Delinquent Boys: The Culture of the Gang.* 1955.

Erikson, K. T.: Notes on the sociology of deviance. *Soc Prob, 9:*308, 1962.

Kitsuse, T. I.: Societal reactions to deviant behavior: Problems of theory and method. *Soc Prob, 9:*253, 1962.

Merton, R. K.: Social structure and anomie. *Am Soc Rev, 3:*572-682, 1938.

Miller, W. B.: Lower class culture is a generating milieu of gang delinquency. *J Soc Issues, 14*(3):5-19, 1958.

Sutherland, E. H. and Cressey, D. R.: *Criminology,* 8th ed. Philadelphia, Lippincott, 1970.

Additional Reading

López Rey, M., Toro Calder, J., Cedeño Zavala, C.: *Extensión, Caracteristicas y Tendencias de la Criminalidad en Puerto Rico.* Puerto Rico, Social Science Research Center, University of Puerto Rico, Rio Piedras Campas.